LEADERSHIP
BY ENCOURAGEMENT

LEADERSHIP
BY ENCOURAGEMENT

by
Don Dinkmeyer, Ph.D. & Daniel Eckstein, Ph.D.

St. Lucie Press
Delray Beach, Florida

Phone: (407) 274-9906
Fax: (407) 274-9927

S$_L^t$

Published by
St. Lucie Press
100 E. Linton Blvd., Suite 403B
Delray Beach, FL 33483

TABLE OF CONTENTS

FOREWORD

If we're a team, how come I'm not on it? This question conveys, perhaps, the most unexpressed feeling in our companies. After reading Dinkmeyer and Eckstein, I think it's clear the answer to this haunting question is that as individuals and organizations, we may not know the meaning of encouragement and surely don't know how to practice it.

Most of us go through life using the word daily. But we use it frothily, employing it in the service of bland, mild support. "I have to encourage Charley to be more punctual."

Put that passive notion away as you read this book. These pages are about people and organizations caring, stretching, engaging, and taking significant emotional risks. To encourage, whether others or ourselves, is to make courageous. I'm convinced that, true to the perversity of human nature, many challenges that frighten us the most are precisely those we find exhilarating when we put our heads down and gut them through. Jacques Maritain, the French theologian and philosopher, wrote "The man of courage flees forward."

Dinkmeyer and Eckstein help us flee forward, and that's nothing but good new for us and our organizations. If we are to add value to our teams, our teams are to add value to the organizations, and our organizations are to add value to our larger world, then we have to learn to give and receive what is uniquely good about ourselves and our associates. In other words, we have to share our gifts.

We know that, for many of us, the workplace is not a climate which enhances the expression of gifts—either those we're confident of or those we haven't refined and are afraid of even trying. The authors know this, too, yet don't allow us to get mired in negativism. They have prescriptions that are specific and workable.

The hands-on practicality of *Leadership by Encouragement* can be found on virtually every page, but let me mention a few features that are particularly outstanding. First of all, each of the eight chapters concludes with a triad made up of (1) key points, (2) applications of leadership by encouragement, and (3) encouragement skills. This triad ensures that the main points are summarized and that the reader isn't left hanging without action steps to take and competencies to develop.

Chapter 5, "Leaders as Encouragers and Motivators," is a gem. It contains a framework for establishing an encouraging system throughout your organization as well as 20 affirmations of the encouraging leader. I assure you if you work at practicing them, you'll change your life and the lives of your associates dramatically for the better, forever. Chapter 4 includes fresh insights and guidelines for conducting positive performance reviews.

The appendix alone is worth the price of admission. There, in a few pages, is a short course for encouraging yourself and others toward distinctive performance. The Encouragement Circle Process is one of its elements you may find helpful. I certainly do.

For a long time, I have believed the effective executive is someone who combines an attention to detail with taking the broad, long view. In a parallel vein, Dinkmeyer and Eckstein have shown their wisdom by giving us a book that reintroduces us to a mega-concept grown common by its familiarity—encouragement—and clarifies how it can be put to uncommon good use.

Allan Cox
Allan Cox & Associates, Inc.

Allan Cox is president of Allan Cox & Associates, Inc., a Chicago-based firm specializing in top management team effectiveness and executive development. He is also a contributing editor to *Success* magazine. His books include *Confessions of a Corporate Head-hunter, The Making of an Achiever, The Cox Report on the American Corporation,* and *Straight Talk for Monday Morning.*

AUTHORS

Don Dinkmeyer, Ph.D., is president of Communication & Motivation Training Institute, Inc. in Coral Springs, Florida. He is a Diplomate in Counseling Psychology and a Diplomate in Family Psychology.

Dr. Dinkmeyer received the Professional Development Award from the American Association for Counseling and Development in 1986 and was named Distinguished Senior Contributor to Counseling Psychology by the American Psychological Association in 1990.

The author of over 150 professional articles and 30 books, Dr. Dinkmeyer has consulted and conducted workshops in 46 states, Canada, Mexico, South America, England, Germany, Switzerland, and Japan.

Daniel Eckstein, Ph.D., is an associate professor of psychology at Ottawa University, Phoenix, and president of the Scottsdale Transcultural Institute. He is also an adjunct associate professor for the Thunderbird American International Graduate School of Management in Glendale, Arizona. He has served as senior consultant with University Associates of San Diego and has also been a consultant with the Atlanta Consulting Group and Hawaii International Institute.

He was a participant in the 1968 Coaches' All-American Football Game and later played two years of professional football with the Green Bay Packers, the Hamilton (Ontario) Tiger-Cats, and the Miami Dolphins.

Dr. Eckstein is co-author of 40 articles and 7 books. He holds a Diplomate in Counseling Psychology from the American Board of Professional Psychologists.

INTRODUCTION

"We live by encouragement and we die without it,
slowly, sadly, and angrily."

Celeste Holme

Webster's defines encouragement as "the act of inspiring others with renewed courage, renewed spirit, or renewed hope." In *Acts of Love: The Power of Encouragement*, David Jeremiah addresses the spiritual foundation supporting the importance of encouragement. He notes that in the New Testament, the word most often translated as encouragement is *parakalein*. It comes from two Greek words: *para*, which means alongside of, and *kaleo*, which means to call. Thus, when people come alongside us during difficult times to give us renewed courage, a renewed spirit, renewed hope—that is encouragement.[1]

William Barclay[2] helps us to understand the historical background of the term:

> "Again and again we find that *Parakalein* is the word of the rallying call; it is the word used in the speeches of leaders and of soldiers who urge each other on. It is...used of words which send fearful and timorous and hesitant soldiers and sailors courageously into battle. A *Parakletos* is therefore an *Encourager*, one who puts courage into the fainthearted, one who nerves the feeble arm for fight, one who makes a very ordinary man cope gallantly with a perilous and a dangerous situation..."

Leadership also needs to be defined. W.F. Ulmer believes that "Leadership is an activity—an influence process—in which an individual gains the trust and commitment of others and without recourse to formal position or authority moves the group to the accomplishment of one or more tasks."[3] Leadership may also be thought of as mobilizing others toward a goal shared by leader and followers.

While there are numerous definitions of leadership, the common element among them is that leadership is a group process which involves interaction between at least two persons in pursuit of a goal. Newer theories of leadership focus on the power of the leader's personality to change workers' goals—to inspire them, provide a model that they want to emulate, and influence them to forsake their own goals and adopt those of the leader. These theories fall under the headings of charismatic or transformational leadership, and they are currently the most intriguing to academics as well as corporate trainers.

James Champy,[4] author of the best-seller *Reengineering the Corporation* and the follow-up *Reengineering Management,*[5] identifies the following four different types of leaders:

1. ***Self-managers***—People who may not think of themselves as managers because, in the last analysis, they answer only for the quality of their own work, such as customer service representatives, researchers, salespeople, lawyers, and accountants

2. ***Process and people managers***—Those who answer for the work of others, usually individuals, a team, or a group of teams working closely with customers or on a specific process

3. ***Expertise managers***—Such as technology managers and managers of human resource development programs

4. ***Enterprise managers***—Such as CEOs, division heads, and those with profit-and-loss responsibility[6]

Most companies today are not doing enough to actively develop and nurture creativity; instead, they are stifling the creative instincts and energy of their people by discouraging risk taking and innovation.

What is needed are people who are capable of motivating and bringing together an organization comprised of a work force that is increasingly diverse in nature, that has less loyalty to its corporate parent, or that has been downsized. What is needed are people who can unite a work force at a time when confidence in leaders and institutions is at an all-time low.

Business needs "shaker-uppers"—people who are capable of working in a chaotic and hectic world. Instead, we have a generation of managers who have been trained to keep things as they are, whereas leadership requires creating something new.[7]

Among leadership theories today, path-goal theory has generated a tremendous amount of interest. The basic idea behind path-goal theory is that in order to produce desired organizational results, certain tasks must be performed. The results are the goal; the tasks are the path. When appropriate, rewards for the individual should be provided. The role of the leader is to (1) ensure that the path toward the goal is clearly understood by subordinates, (2) reduce barriers to the achievement of the goal, and (3) increase the number of personal payoffs to subordinates for attaining the goal.[8]

Leaders who hope to retain their jobs in a changing economy must learn to alter the nature of power and how it is utilized. What has been called "virtual leadership"[9] is based on such changing technologies as portable modules built around information networks, flexible work forces and work hours, outsourcing, and webs of strategic partnerships.

As position power continues to erode, corporate leaders resemble candidates running for office in contrast to the former captains of ships. Today, leaders face two formidable challenges. The first is to develop and articulate what the company is trying to accomplish. The second is to allow employees to determine both specific customer and job needs and how to effectively meet them.

Executives who rose to prominence in traditional systems often have difficulty in both areas. Their quantitative skills do not help them communicate, and their high intelligence, energy, ambition, and self-confidence are often perceived as arrogance, which further alienates them from other workers.

Emergent "virtual leaders" are changing the heroic, independent "lone wolf, "I must do it all by myself" syndrome. They know they cannot solve all the problems themselves and instead stress teamwork in an increasingly diverse, multicultural workplace. They also "walk the walk" and "talk the talk" by modeling and practicing what they preach.

In the past, a company could almost be run without a leader at the top through the efforts of highly efficient middle managers who operated by the book and by the numbers. As technology and the economy made many middle managers obsolete, many corporations "flattened" their hierarchical structures by pushing the former traditional management tasks down the line to workers. With middle management virtually eliminated, upper management is now confronted with severe leadership challenges.[10]

Like the dinosaurs, companies that cannot adapt are becoming fossils. And like the wild western frontier of the 1800s, many new upstart entrepreneurs are revolutionizing how business is being conducted. For example, instead of a 9- to 12-month waiting period for a published book, instant documentaries now appear on the newsstands within one or two weeks following such sensational stories as the O.J. Simpson case. Instant telecommunications now make it possible to ship your data halfway around the world, have it processed more cheaply during someone else's daylight hours while you sleep, and have it back when you arise the next morning.

In *Emotional Intelligence,* Daniel Coleman, behavioral reporter for the *New York Times,* writes that at best, IQ contributes only 20 percent to the factors that determine life success. He believes that many people with a high IQ actually work for people of much "lower" IQ who have what he calls higher "emotional intelligence" (EQ).[11]

Successful leaders are those who can cooperate, persuade, empathize with others, and build consensus. One study found that the true stars in a think tank of engineers were those who could tap into the informal communications network during a crisis and get quick responses to their e–mail questions.

Leadership by encouragement is one of the practical interpersonal "people" skills that can help raise one's "EQ." It is a practical approach that characterizes "smart" leaders.

> "Ninety-five percent of American managers today
> say the right thing. Five percent actually do it."
>
> James O'Toole

This is a book about leadership. Being a leader is not defined by one's vertical position in the organizational chart. True leadership is often more truly demonstrated at the lower levels of the company pecking order. While the examples in this book focus primarily on business-oriented situations, leaders in all aspects of life, including home, school, church or synagogue, volunteer and service agencies, mental health agencies, etc., can benefit from the generic skill of encouragement, which is the corner-stone of this book. Indeed, many of the basic ideas originated in the child guidance, family counseling, and class discipline theories espoused by Alfred Adler and Rudolf Dreikurs in the early and middle part of this century.

This book is organized to move the reader from a general overview of leadership in organizations to a *specific* description of the who, what, when, where, and why of the subtle philosophy and the demonstrable skill of encouragement. Thus, the first part of the book (Chapters 1 and 2) lays a broad-based foundation relative to the value of human capital; this is followed in Chapter 3 by a specific theoretical approach to the psychology of work, namely the works originated by Alfred Adler and Rudolf Dreikurs. Chapter 4 introduces a developmental model which the authors call the improving managerial performance cycle. An encouraging approach to confrontation and firing is featured. The remaining chapters deal specifically with encouragement theory. Suggested group activities are included in the Appendix to further make encouragement a concrete reality in a company.

Each chapter concludes with a triad made up of (1) key points, (2) applications of leadership by encouragement, and (3) encouragement skills. Each triad summarizes the main points in the chapter and provides the reader with action steps for putting the theory into practice.

One way to define what encouragement is would be to illustrate what it is *not*. For example, specific characteristics of discouraging leaders are presented in Chapter 5. Such subtle methods of discouragement as domination, insensitivity, silence, and intimidation are defined and illustrated. Discouragement is then contrasted with specific characteristics and illustrations of encouraging leaders.

Let's once again address the "95 percent *talk* versus 5 percent *do*" discrepancy by briefly illustrating what encouragement is *not* for the purposes of this overview to the book. Many managers believe that they are encouraging simply because they use the word in a sentence. For example, one manager said in a loud, harsh tone of voice while simultaneously pounding his fist on the table, "You're damn straight I'm encouraging...I encourage my workers to get the job done by noon or they're fired!"

A second example of what encouragement is not is illustrated by one aspect of the coaching philosophy of Buddy Ryan, head coach of the NFL Arizona Cardinals. He brags that a core component of what he calls "Buddyball" is "*my* way or the highway!" If intimidation and domination are your preferred mode of management style, then read no further, for you have the wrong book.

> "It is not the employer who pays the wages.
> Employers only handle money.
> It is the customer who pays the wages."
>
> Henry Ford

Encouragement sometimes involves confrontation. The "tough love" philosophy can involve hurting someone's feelings by telling the truth, no matter how painful. Encouragement is not false flattery that seeks to "pump up" employees. In Chapter 4, we will focus on an encouraging approach to conflict and confrontation. Physically or emotionally "holding" someone in order to avoid hurtful situations or to "make it better" for an employee who consistently falls below an acceptable job performance standard is not empowerment. There is a more encouraging approach to such challenging situations which includes compassion and basic respect. Thus, to encourage is not to be dishonest or to engage in vain flattery. It is to empower by being honest in a respectful way.

Just as "the customer is always right," so too is encouragement only encouraging to the extent to which the receiver of a communication, or the worker, feels that the message delivered is in fact encouraging. A message such as "I'm a great encourager…it's those ungrateful workers who just don't get it" doesn't wash here as encouragement. When a worker, whether rightly or wrongly, receives a communication in a discouraging manner, then the responsibility lies with the leader, not the worker, to change his or her approach.

Chapter 6 further explores this concept by addressing the method and procedures of encouragement training. The specific competencies of attending, listening, responding, demonstrating empathy, identifying similarities, seeing perceptual alternatives, developing responsibility and productivity in others, plus leadership from the heart all are identified as concrete encouragement training skills. A linguistic model of workplace communication is also included.

> "Good management is largely a matter of love. Or if you're uncomfortable with that word, call it caring, because proper management involves caring for people, not manipulating them."
>
> James Autry

Chapter 7 addresses the philosophy of participative management coupled with specific suggestions and strategies for organizations to be more encouraging. A section of Chapter 8 is devoted to the theory and practice of team building as an interpersonal skills learning intervention. This chapter also summarizes and explores relevant recommended next steps, additional sources of information, and possible seminars/workshops.

The Appendix contains 16 specific group and individual activities of encouragement which leaders can actually implement. For example, such activities as assessing encouraging leaders, evaluating your leadership relationships, the encouragement circle process, performance review, and asset focusing are all meant to be practiced. They are "where the rubber meets the road" activities which can be applied within the workplace.

A variety of self-assessment questionnaires which are designed to get the reader actively involved and to provide personal feedback on encouragement appear throughout the book. Questionnaires such as "You as an Encouraging Leader," "Your Leadership Style," and "Performance Coaching" supplement action steps by providing specific feedback. At other times, the reader is invited to respond to open-ended questions. Comparing one's family of origin to one's current workplace is another example of actively involving the reader in the process.

Although this book is organized from a general to a specific deductive perspective, each chapter is self-contained. Thus, it is not necessary to read Chapters 1, 2, 3, etc. in that order. The reader is invited to find the portion of the book that is most personally relevant and begin there.

> "**W**ork is a four-letter word. It's up to us to decide whether that four-letter word reads 'drag' or 'love.' Most work is a drag because it doesn't nourish our souls. The key is to trust your heart to move where your talents can flourish. This old world will really spin when work becomes a joyous expression of the soul."
>
> Al Sacharov

The primary purpose of this book is to provide specific, practical, proven suggestions that can help reduce the 95 percent of leaders who *talk* the right words versus the 5 percent who actually *do* encourage others. This book provides a broad-based theory of human relations theory and then moves to one essential ingredient of effective leadership—encouragement.

THE ESSENCE OF THE ENCOURAGING LEADER

Encouraging Leaders =
Encouraged Employees =
An Encouraged Organization =
Appreciated Customers

Encouragement is a process that focuses on the individual's resources and potential in order to enhance self-esteem and self-acceptance. Discouragement is based on lack of belief in one's abilities to find solutions and to make some positive movement. Encouragement is strongly correlated with an optimistic philosophy of life, whereas discouragement is too often synonymous with pessimism.

The psychological basis of discouragement involves high standards, expectations of perfection, feelings of inadequacy, and doubt in one's abilities. The courageous person, on the other hand, is motivated, energized, and involved; takes risks for meaningful reasons; says "yes" to self; sees problems as challenges; and has self-esteem and self-acceptance.

Specific skills for encouraging leaders include:

- Listening
- Reflecting feelings
- Giving feedback
- Focusing on strengths and resources
- Developing perceptual alternatives
- Utilizing humor to keep perspective
- Identifying similarities
- Focusing on efforts and contributions
- Identifying and combating discouraging fictional beliefs
- Encouraging commitment and movement
- Improving self-encouragement and mental skills
- Dealing with one's own discouragement as one way of modeling a personal commitment to an optimistic philosophy of encouragement

Encouraging leaders:

1. See situations as challenges and opportunities instead of problems
2. Identify the positive potential in every person and every situation
3. Respect and value uniqueness and individual differences
4. Communicate recognition of individual movement, progress, and contributions
5. Communicate openly and honestly
6. See themselves as equal to others in worth and dignity and therefore treat bosses, colleagues, and subordinates as equal participants in the process
7. Provide positive performance reviews
8. Communicate in a language of equality through collaboration, cooperation, agreement, and win–win relationships

9. Facilitate open communication of short- and long-term company goals or mission statements

10. Are committed to giving and receiving feedback

Methods of encouraging leaders:

1. Communicating positive expectations and beliefs

2. Consistently working to build employees' self-esteem

3. Recognizing effort and improvement

4. Utilizing the improving management productivity cycle:
   A. Issue identification
      - Skills
      - Motivation
      - Both skills and motivation
   B. Asset inventory: developing perceptual alternatives
   C. Goal setting and goal alignment
   D. Performance appraisal
   E. Consequences

The encouraging organization:

- Builds trust, open feedback, and honest sharing of opinions
- Provides and communicates a shared vision
- Makes decisions at the point of maximum meaningful input
- Empowers associates
- Believes and practices equality
- Has a horizontal as opposed to vertical hierarchy
- Identifies teams rather than individuals

"The music exists and it doesn't. It is written on the page, but it means nothing until performed and heard. The best leaders, like the best music, inspire us to see new possibilities."
Max DePree

Leadership by encouragement is a way to produce motivated, energized, and involved employees while being a self-motivating, energizing, and rewarding leader. This book is intended to present work-related principles using practical applications of the behavioral sciences. In addition to providing specific guidelines for leadership which can be implemented at home, in school, in government, and in other organizations, it is intended to provide consultants in the applied behavioral sciences with specific intervention strategies that are sought in growing numbers by organizations around the world.

> "**W**hen the great leader has done his work,
> the people will say 'we did it ourselves.'"
>
> Lao Tzu
> (in the fifth century B.C.)

ENCOURAGEMENT AND LEADERSHIP

To encourage is to be a leader who, quietly and often unnoticed and unappreciated, makes a difference by manifesting a positive belief in others. Although being an encouraging person just makes good sense, we will demonstrate specific, concrete examples of such a vital yet often underutilized leadership skill.

The value of encouragement is often taken for granted or missed completely because it tends to be private rather than public. Although there are identifiable words and behaviors correlated with encouragement, in many ways it is best manifested by an attitude that nonverbally communicates caring and compassion.

> "**T**he softest things in the world
> overcome the hardest things in the world."
>
> Lao Tzu

Encouragement is a process that focuses on the individual's resources and potential to assist in building self-esteem and self-confidence. Encouragement is a theory that becomes a reality through application of the skills essential for establishing courage and confidence.

Encouraging leaders apply basic skills such as:

- Listening attentively
- Responding empathically
- Providing respect and enthusiasm
- Focusing on strengths and resources

- Seeing positive alternatives for any trait

- Viewing challenges with humor and in perspective

An article titled "The Leader as Servant" relates closely to the philosophy of the encouraging leader. Servant leaders have the following characteristics:

1. They take people and their work really, really seriously. This is more than empowerment. It is accepting human beings as having value in their own right.

2. They listen and take their lead from the "troops." Such leaders don't always have answers; often they have pertinent questions. The answers come from the people working with customers.

3. They heal. They are vulnerable, open, and willing to share in mistakes while acknowledging and encouraging continuously.

4. They are self-effacing and avoid drawing attention to themselves. They do not seek praise or to appear to be the reason for success.

5. They see themselves as stewards.[12]

Max DePree and Sam Walton, elected to the Business Hall of Fame in 1992, demonstrated that a caring, encouraging environment and commercial success can be combined. DePree was CEO of Herman Miller, a company whose sales increased 220 percent from 1980 to 1987 and which was listed in the *Fortune* survey as one of the most admired corporations in the United States. DePree practiced the leader-as-a-servant philosophy and demonstrated the ability to walk his talk; his leadership reflected his beliefs.

Sam Walton, founder of Wal-Mart, revolutionized retailing as he accomplished his two major goals: provide the lowest prices to customers and provide the highest level of motivation to employees. Jack Welch, CEO of General Electric, visited Wal-Mart management sessions and said, "Everyone there has a passion for an idea, and everybody's idea counts. Hierarchy doesn't matter. They get eighty people in a room and understand how to deal with each other without structure." Sam Walton told *USA Today* about this philosophy of employees as associates about a year before his death: "You have to talk to people. You have to listen to them, mostly. You have to make them know this is a partnership."[13]

"It's what you learn after you know it all that counts."

John Wooden

To be an effective leader, one should engage in continual self-reflection and self-renewal. In *Leadership and the Customer Revolution,* Heil, Parker, and Tate suggest that effective leaders should focus on answers to such questions as:

- What have I learned lately?

- In the last six months, what have I changed my mind about?

- When was the last time my assumptions were dead wrong?

- What is different about the way I think this year?

- What about my present mindset have I found myself questioning recently?

- What have I learned this month that makes my action last month seem less effective?

- Who thinks very differently than I do? What have I learned from them lately?

- How much time have I spent in the last month questioning the way I think and the structures I have designed to support improvement?[14]

"You teach best what you most need to learn," says Richard Bach, author of *Jonathan Livingston Seagull,* in his book *Illusions.*[15] It has been a challenging process for us to develop this book over an extended period of time. The untimely death of Doug Blocksma, our original co-author, was a major sadness for us. Writing about encouragement was a journey for us as organizational consultants, as we explored the discouraging, shadowy aspects of our own personal and professional selves.

It is with a sense of humility that we introduce a book on such a profound topic as encouragement. We hope to model that encouragement is not an ultimate destination but rather a continual commitment to improvement, despite our own human shortcomings.

> *Zen student:* "Master, what is Zen?"
>
> *Master:* "Zen is eating when you eat, working when you work, and relaxing when you relax."
>
> *Zen student:* "But, Master, that is so simple!"
>
> *Master:* "Yes, but so few people do it."

Leadership by encouragement begins with a commitment to *encourage oneself first*. None of us is perfect. Encouragement is the commitment to practice continually, to receive ongoing coaching and feedback, and to seek continual improvement by dedicating oneself to one's best effort. Such an approach can improve our own encouragement/discouragement "batting average."

> "**R**espect, loyalty, security, dignity—old-fashioned qualities for a new-fashioned economy. Earlier this century machines helped liberate our ancestors from the toil of the fields. In this generation, wondrous technology has freed us from the drudgery of the assembly line and enabled us to speed new products to far-off markets. As we approach the millennium, it is people who will carry us forward. In an economy built on service, the extent to which we prosper will depend on our ability to educate, entertain, empower, and ennoble ourselves—and each other."
>
> *Fortune*

Regardless of one's political, religious, or philosophic orientation, we believe that encouragement is the path of the heart—a universal symbol of caring and compassion. We hope that this book will make a positive contribution in helping to stimulate other creative approaches and ideas on encouragement. We welcome others' ideas in helping to refine and illustrate the encouragement process in action.

A new millennium dawns before us. As in previous eras, those who cling to the past often become rigid and dogmatic, unable to adapt to change. It is the visionaries, the pioneers who forge ahead, who are most likely to claim the rewards of the future. This book is written for the pathfinders who are seeking another positive step in the pursuit of their dreams of a better life for themselves and for others. Improving the quality of the world of work through the utilization of the profoundly simple concept of encouragement is one of the practical ways of making such dreams a reality.

The Credit Belongs

The credit belongs to those who
Are actually in the arena, who strive
Valiantly, who know the great
Enthusiasms, the great devotions
And spend themselves in a worthy cause.
Who at the best, know the triumph

Of high achievement, and who,
At the worst, if they fail, fail
While daring greatly, so that their
Place shall never be with those cold
And timid souls who know neither
Victory or defeat.

Theodore Roosevelt

REFERENCES

1. Jeremiah, D., *Acts of Love: The Power of Encouragement,* Gresham, OR: Vision House, 1994.

2. Barclay, W., *New Testament Words,* Philadelphia: Westminster Press, 1994, p. 221.

3. Clark, K., Clark, M., and Campbell, K., *Impact of Leadership,* Greensboro, NC: Center for Creative Leadership, p. 2.

4. Champy, J., *Reengineering the Corporation,* New York: Harper & Collins, 1993, p. 93.

5. Champy, J., *Reengineering Management,* New York: Harper & Collins, 1995, p. 95.

6. Champy, J., *Reengineering Management,* New York: Harper & Collins, 1995, p. 4.

7. Wills, G., "What makes a good leader?" *The Atlantic,* 273(4), April 1994, p. 63.

8. Price, R., "An investment of path-goal leadership theory of marketing." *Journal of Retailing,* September 1991.

9. Capowski, G., "Anatomy of a leader: where are the leaders of tomorrow?" *Management Review,* March 1994.

10. Huey, J., "The new post-heroic leadership." *Fortune,* February 21, 1994, p. 42.

11. Coleman, Daniel, *Emotional Intelligence,* New York: Bantam, 1995.

12. Kiechel, N., "The leader as servant." *Fortune,* May 4, 1992, pp. 121–122.

13. Neuborne, E., "Mr. Sam's secret." *USA Today,* April 6, 1992, p. 18.

14. Heil, G., Parks, T., and Tate, R., *Leadership and the Customer Revolution,* New York: Van Nostrand Reinhold, 1995.

15. Bach, R., *Illusions,* New York: Dell, 1977.

1

THE PSYCHOLOGY OF ENCOURAGEMENT

"The key element in good business management
is emotional attitude. The rest is mechanics."

Harold Geeneen

INTRODUCTION TO ENCOURAGEMENT

The most basic concepts are too often taken for granted, ignored, or dismissed as simplistic. The changing and challenging role of manager requires new standards of excellence. In fact, the very term "manager," symbolic of a dictatorial, autocratic, controlling style, is dying. Like the legendary phoenix, a new bird, "leader," is emerging from the ashes.

Leadership by encouragement is one of the core strategies in positively motivating employees toward increased productivity.

"Every vital organization
thrives because it depends more
on commitment and enthusiasm
than on the letter of the contract."

Max DePree

WHAT IS LEADERSHIP?

Kern summarizes the research on effective leadership in the following nine statements:

1. Good leaders pay attention to both task and relationship behaviors.
2. Behavioral descriptions can improve a leader's effectiveness.
3. Leaders can be trained; they are not merely born that way.
4. Intelligence becomes a factor as people move up the organizational chart.
5. As stress increases, it interferes with effective leadership.
6. Feedback from others is important in developing leaders.
7. Good leaders account for a 25 percent increase in productivity.
8. There is no evidence to indicate any significant difference between good male and female leaders.
9. Leader/follower compatibility dictates success.[1]

WHAT IS ENCOURAGEMENT?

Encouragement is the process whereby one focuses on the individual's resources in order to build that person's self-esteem, self-confidence, and feelings of worth. Encouragement involves focusing on any resource that can be turned into an asset or strength.

Dinkmeyer and Losoncy[2] define encouragement as:

> "...The process of facilitating the development of a person's inner resources and courage towards positive movement. The encouraging person helps the discouraged person remove some of the self-imposed roadblocks. The goal of encouragement, then, is to aid the individual to move from a philosophy that suggests 'I can't' to the more productive 'I will.'"

Specifically, the shift from discouraged to more encouraged beliefs and behaviors is moving from being "turned off" (discouraged) to being "turned on" (encouraged). Specific examples are the changes from "I can't" and "I won't" to "I can" and "I will" and "I am." Other examples of such a discouraged/encouraged polarity are stagnant/growing, irresponsible/responsible, helpless/significant, opinionated/flexible, and energy-misdirected/energy-directed.

According to psychiatrist Rudolf Dreikurs, humans need encouragement much as plants need water. He believed that every person with whom one comes in contact feels better or worse based on how others behave toward him or her. Dreikurs said, "We constantly encourage or discourage those around us and thereby contribute materially to their greater or lesser ability to function."[3]

> "...The difference between a lady and a flower girl is not how she behaves but how she's treated. I shall always be a flower girl to Professor Higgins because he always treats me as a flower girl and always will; but I know I can be a lady to you because you always treat me as a lady and always will."
>
> Eliza Doolittle
> in George Bernard Shaw's *Pygmalion*

A certain philosophy or psychology serves as the foundation upon which the decision to be encouraging is built. It can be illustrated by a classic question: Is the glass half full or is the glass half empty? For an optimistic, encouraged person, the answer is half full, which indicates positive movement toward becoming more full. Conversely, a pessimistic, discouraged answer indicates a deficit-oriented, "half-empty" approach.

In *Love Is Letting Go of Fear,* Gerald Jampolsky suggests that there are only two basic emotions: love (which could be characterized as being encouraged) and fear (discouraged).[4] A philosophy/psychology of encouragement is based on the belief that it is human nature to be more encouraged than discouraged.

In *Carl Rogers on Personal Power,* the founder of client-centered therapy recalls his family's winter supply of potatoes, stored several feet below a small basement window. Despite unfavorable conditions, the potatoes would begin to sprout. Although they were white, unlike the healthy green shoots that emerge from springtime soil, those pale basement sprouts grew two to three feet as they reached for the distant light above them. Rogers realized that, "They were, in their bizarre fertile growth, a sort of desperate expression of the directional tendency...they would never become a plant, never mature, never fulfill their real potentiality. But under the most adverse circumstances, they were striving to become. Life would not give up, even if it could not flourish."[5]

The idea that we are all created with a spark of divinity within us reflects an encouraging philosophy of life; it hints that we can better ourselves and the world through personal growth and societal transformation.

THE HALF-EMPTY VERSUS HALF-FULL
PHILOSOPHY OF LIFE

*"E*nthusiasm is contagious. It's difficult to remain neutral
or indifferent in the presence of a positive thinker."

Denis Waitley and Remi Witt

Psychologist Martin Seligman made a profound contribution to the study
of what he calls "learned helplessness." Seligman believes that each of us
carries a word in our heart.

*"F*or some of us that word is 'yes.' Yes, we believe we can succeed.
Yes, we can learn. Yes, we can make a difference. Others carry a
'no,' with all the negative baggage that accompanies it. As leaders,
we must realize which word we carry and how it enhances or
inhibits our ability to lead. Skills and desire are not enough to
succeed. We must also be convinced that we *can*...and be able to
convince others, as well. If we are passionately optimistic, odds are
that our optimism will be contagious."

Learned Optimism (p. 256)

For the past two decades, Seligman has focused his research on how
to be more proactive in life. In his best-seller *Learned Optimism*, he
presents many research articles that indicate profound differences between
an optimistic (encouraged) philosophy and a more pessimistic (discouraged) one. His seminal work lends new credence to important differences
in the "half-full versus half-empty" approaches to life's challenges.[6]

Fundamental psychological differences exist between optimistic and
pessimistic orientations. The core belief of pessimists is "learned helplessness," or the belief that nothing they do can change their situation, that
many things are simply beyond their control, and that others run their
lives. The cognitive psychologist Albert Ellis devised the ABC model to
explain that it is not an event (A = activating event) that causes a
consequence (C), but rather a belief (B). For example, a poor performance
rating does not cause an employee to be depressed. Instead, an intervening belief (e.g., "I am a failure") triggers the reaction. The encouraging
aspect of cognitive therapy is that beliefs are subjective and the individual
has the power to change them. Thus, beliefs can and often must be shifted
from a discouraged, pessimistic style to an encouraged, optimistic one.[7]

*"N*o one really knows enough to be a pessimist."

Norman Cousins

> "**I** am convinced that life is 10% what happens to me and 90% how I react to it. And so it is with you. We are in charge of our attitudes."
>
> Charles Swindoll

> "**L**ife inflicts the same setbacks and tragedies on the optimist as on the pessimist, but the optimist weathers them better. As we have seen, the optimist bounces back from defeat, and, with his life somewhat poorer, he picks up and starts again. The pessimist gives up and falls into depression. Because of his resilience, the optimist achieves more at work, at school, and on the playing field. The optimist has better physical health and may even live longer. Americans want optimists to lead them. Even when things go well for the pessimist, he is haunted by foreboding of catastrophe."
>
> Martin Seligman

Seligman identified three pivotal dimensions of an optimistic orientation: *permanence, pervasiveness,* and *personalization.* Encouraged, optimistic leaders resist helplessness by believing that the causes of bad events are temporary, localized, and not related to their self-worth. Discouraged, pessimistic leaders believe that the causes of bad events are permanent, pervasive, and somehow connected to them.

The following are some examples of the permanence dimension:

Permanent (Pessimistic)	*Temporary (Optimistic)*
"Our suppliers never get us our materials on time."	"We recently had a challenging time getting needed supplies."
"My boss is always nagging me."	"My boss gets really frustrated when my reports are late."
"I just can't keep up with this job."	"This is an especially challenging time right now."

The permanence dimension of optimism has just the opposite effect in explaining good events. Leaders who believe that good events have permanent causes are more optimistic than those who believe that they have temporary ones.

Temporary (Pessimistic)	*Permanent (Optimistic)*
"Sometimes I am able to solve problems on the job."	"I'm good at finding solutions to work problems."

| "Our department produced its quota for a change." | "We have a great department that is able to meet its sales quotas." |

Whereas permanence relates to time, pervasiveness, a second key factor, relates to space. Global or universal explanations for failure cause the problem to be transferred into other areas of one's life.

Universal (Pessimistic)	*Specific (Optimistic)*
"All CEOs are arrogant, aloof, and unconcerned about the worker."	"Our CEO is more concerned with numbers and the technical aspects of the company than with people."
"The computers always go down just when we need them."	"Since the computers are down, we can't work on the primary project. What other priorities can we attend to in the meantime?"

The final aspect of an optimistic style is *personalization.* Low self-esteem generally comes from responding to bad events with internal blaming. Examples of such responses are "I am really stupid for losing that account" or "I just can't be honest with my boss concerning my reservations about her proposal."[6]

"If you think you're beaten, you are,
If you think you dare not, you don't.
If you'd like to win, but think you can't
It's almost a cinch you won't.

If you think you'll lose, you've lost
For out in the world you'll find
Success begins with a fellow's will.
It's all in a state of mind.

Full many a game is lost
'er 'ere a play is run
And many a coward fails
'er 'ere his work's begun.

Think big, and your deeds will grow.
Think small, and you'll lag behind.
Think you can, and you will;
It's all in a state of mind.

If you think you're outclassed, you are.
You've got to think high to rise,
You've got to be sure of yourself,
Before you can win a prize.

Life's battles don't always go
To the stronger or faster man,
But soon or late, the man who wins
Is the fellow who thinks he can."

Anon

Earlier in the chapter, the ABC model of Ellis was introduced, where A = activating events or adversity, B = beliefs, and C = consequence (or feelings). Seligman expands this model into the ABCDE approach by adding D = disputation and E = energization.

Disputation uses questions of *evidence* ("show me"), *alternatives* (focusing on the changeable), *implications* (decatastrophize the horrible, irreparable situation into an unpleasant, fixable one), and *usefulness* ("Is the belief destructive?" and "What is the payoff of this attitude for me?").

Energization comes from disputing discouraging, self-condemning thoughts. It is the reward for making positive changes in one's life.[6]

Consider the following situation:

A. **Adversity**—"My quarterly performance review with the vice president was completed yesterday. She noted that employee morale in my unit seems low. She also described my reports as brief, incomplete, and often inadequate in addressing our targeted performance objectives."

B. **Belief**—"I am a failure. I am probably going to get fired."

C. **Consequences**—"I feel worried and anxious, and I doubt my abilities to handle my management responsibilities. I fear being replaced because at age 54 I probably can't get another job. My family is counting on me to provide for them. I also feel angry at my boss for what I feel is overly harsh criticism."

D. **Disputation**—"Several strengths were noted in my review, especially in the areas of advertising and marketing. Granted, my reports have not been adequate, but I am certainly capable of doing them better. I will commit to reviewing the performance standards and addressing them more specifically. Low employee morale could be due factors other than my leadership. Being fired is highly unlikely given my overall favorable evaluation. Even if I were fired, my spouse and other family members can contribute to our total income. I am also blaming my boss unfairly; that is how she sees my performance. I'll work hard to change her opinion."

E. ***Energization***—"I feel bad about these areas of deficiency because I pride myself on excellence. I would prefer a higher evaluation but I've also been down on myself, which has caused my production to drop off even more. Although I was initially depressed about this, actually it has had a positive effect in motivating me to improve our department, and I've gotten some specific areas to focus my efforts on. I *can* and *will* improve!"

Now you are invited to record two specific examples of your own ABCDE encouraging, optimistic leadership commitment.

Event One:

Adversity:_____

Belief:_____

Consequences:_____

Disputation:_____

Energization:_____

Event Two:

Adversity:_____

Belief:_____

Consequences:_____

Disputation:_____

Energization:_____

CREATING A POSITIVE MENTAL ATTITUDE

"**K**eep your face in the sunshine and you cannot see a shadow."

Helen Keller

Dale Carnegie, author of the best-seller *How to Win Friends & Influence People,* was once asked on a radio program to tell in three sentences the most important lesson he had ever learned. He replied that it was "the stupendous importance of what we think. If I knew what you think, I would know who you are, for your thoughts make you what you are. By changing our thoughts, we can change our lives."[8]

ABUNDANCE MANAGERS

In *Principle-Centered Leadership,* Stephen Covey expands on the wisdom presented in his best-seller *The Seven Habits of Highly Effective People.* What he calls "abundance management" is closely correlated with encouraging leadership. He defines "abundance mentality" as a bone-deep belief that "there are enough natural and human resources to realize my dream" and that "my success does not necessarily mean failure for others, just as their success does not preclude my own."

A contrasting "scarcity mentality" emerges from a belief that resources are limited. Such a belief results in a win–lose approach to business and interpersonal relationships because there is only so much of anything to go around.

Covey specifically identifies the following seven characteristics of abundance managers:

1. They return often to the right sources (that being a sense of internal security), sources that keep them gentle, open, trusting, and genuinely happy for the successes of other people.

2. They seek solitude and enjoy nature.

3. They "sharpen the saw" regularly, meaning that they continue their education by continually exercising their minds and bodies.

4. They serve others anonymously.

5. They maintain a long-term, intimate relationship with another person.

6. They forgive themselves and others.

7. They are problem solvers, specifically being able to separate the people from the problem being addressed.[9]

Coupled with a half-full approach, abundance managers believe that the universe is truly one of plenty rather than scarcity. Such an internal source of security allows them to approach workers in an encouraging manner. Too often, the very strengths and assets that employees manifest on the job are actively denied and discouraged because they are viewed as threats to the boss. A leader who believes that his or her subordinates can succeed only at his or her expense will be threatened by successes within the unit. Abundance managers are secure enough within themselves to be able to hire and "cultivate" first-rate people because their own identities are not adversely affected. Thus, encouragement begins with a philosophy of abundance and optimism.

> "Surround yourself with the highest caliber people. Remember that first rate people hire first rate people—while second rate people hire third rate people."
>
> Richard White, Jr.

A CASE STUDY

The above quote accurately identifies the *systems* implications that an approach to encouragement and empowerment has for consultants and leaders. Within organizations, the success of one person is often viewed with jealousy or envy by others. Any change suggested by leaders can be for better or for worse. Basically, having the courage to change any existing situation always carries a risk. Even when one is successful, there may also be negative consequences. Just as a failure carries the risk of being fired or demoted, so too do encouragement and empowering policies carry the risk of being "too successful" and outshining the boss.

The following case study has been provided by Phyliss Cooke, a San Diego based organizational consultant. She correctly describes it as a story that is "just popping with kernels of wisdom." Here is her first-person account of an intervention where an initial success led to challenges with her client's boss and eventual failure.

> It all started with a call I received a few years ago asking if I was interested in taking on a rather open-ended assignment in my area of expertise, in a Pacific Rim country (that shall remain unnamed), for a major (foreign owned) airline (that shall also remain unnamed), to work with a recently employed junior trainer who needed to be "coached" in order that his "raw talent" could be enhanced, harnessed, and applied to an exciting new training project that he would be heading. It sounded intriguing.
>
> I met with the Human Resource Department (HRD) manager to learn more about their system, the department, the goals of the project, about my client, and to clarify the manager's expectations and the latitudes that I would have in working on the project.
>
> I learned that in the six months that my client to-be had been

on board, he had proven to be somewhat difficult to control, was thought to be fairly undisciplined in following department procedures, was a little lax in completing assigned tasks, etc. On the plus side, his colleagues in the department liked him, and his trainees had given him high marks in the courses that he had led so far, so his manager was still mostly positive about his eventual fit with the department's needs.

My client was being given this new opportunity because his manager thought that while he needed grooming, he was the best person for this project...he had the "right stuff" for the job. It was to be an experiment...to provide a highly experiential training program suitable for large groups of lower level trainees, all of whom had in the past received very little training, except that which was directly related to their tasks.

During my meeting with the (HRD) manager it became clear to me that while his role required him to be responsible for meeting the needs of all employees, even those on the lowest levels, I was speaking with someone who personally believed that the most HRD impact was realized from working with the top levels in the system. (Somewhat elitist, condescending even, but what the heck, he was inviting me to work on something that I believed in, so what difference would it make?)

I then met with my client and found that he fit the descriptions that I had heard of him perfectly...and we hit it off right away.

He was bright, funny, motivated to learn, and skilled in communicating. His previous experience as a trainer had been limited, but it had been in conducting the type of physical activities that would form the basic thrust of the program that we would be designing together, and he knew that this had been the sole basis of his having been hired. In his view, the system needed him more than he needed this job, but he appreciated the opportunity he was being given.

We discussed what he expected from our collaboration...developing his ability to design a training program, learning how to transfer his ideas to others, how to process learning, and how to facilitate in a large group of trainees. He thought that he could pick up these skills fairly quickly, and he knew that he had already learned what many trainers *rely* upon, i.e., how to compensate for the skills he lacked through the force of his personality and his charismatic style.

He was young and somewhat impatient with those who didn't "live life with gusto, taking chances and learning from their mistakes, rather than playing it safe." He realized that he lacked experience in working effectively in a large organization (like this one, very political, with formal structures and practices), but he didn't much care if or how he might fit in in the long-term, as long as he was given a clear mandate to deliver on this project and reassured that we would be free to make all of the decisions.

He told me that he had been vocal about his dissatisfactions with the department and that he believed that he was being given this project to keep him happy and to allow him to "show his stuff." He thought that with my help we could really make an impact and that "it would be fun...the way work should be."

Sounds ideal, right? Well, your warning bells might have gone off sooner than mine did, but what I heard was the sweet sound of a "doable" contract, an opportunity to bring on-line a creative program, to work in a world-class organization in an exotic setting, with the added bonus of being able to help develop the talent of someone just starting out. His manager wanted him to succeed and was providing him with a personal mentor, a resource person who could "jump start" this project. What could possibly be better than that?

As it turned out, our work together and the program we developed were blazing success, yet the whole thing died a premature death. In 18 months we went from a cold start, through concept, research, design, and preparation of training materials, to construction of a ropes course on our training site for the outdoor activities that were included in our program, to development of a training staff, a pilot program, and three scheduled sessions of a wildly successful, well-publicized "team spirit" training program. Then the HRD manager killed the project. So what went wrong?

It wasn't a lack of funding. The president of the airline actually proposed that the HRD budget be increased and the program schedule be revised so that our program could be offered once a month instead of only once a quarter. He had visited the site for the pilot and for each of the three programs that had been conducted and had seen for himself the positive impact that the training was having, that the trainees were appreciative and really enthusiastic, and that following the training they were applying their learning back on the job to resolve many of the small problems that had previously been identified as "lack of motivation" or involving "cultural diversity" issues.

It wasn't that the trainees were reluctant to sign up or that their managers were hesitant to release them for the program. Managers reported high satisfaction with returning trainees' on-the-job performance, and a waiting list quickly filled for the future programs which were scheduled two years in advance. (At 80 to 100 per session, it would have been possible to put all 1200 target employees through even if the program had kept to the quarterly schedule first envisioned.)

It wasn't the cost of the program. Even considering the high initial cost related to the start up, the cost per trainee was less than half of the cost of other programs being offered.

In addition, other trainers in the department were reducing cost and their reliance upon outside consulting resources and vendors by utilizing the skills they had acquired and converting to training designs and materials developed in-house. (These training officers had been included in the professional development programs that had been conducted as part of my client's "coaching" and were part of the pilot group of trainees for our team spirit program.)

Morale in the department was high...there was a new esprit de corps...we were feeling terrific! So what went wrong? All of the above.

We didn't pay attention to the larger system issues that were affected by our apparent successes. Though his department looked good, the HRD manager's sense of importance was being eclipsed by the success of the program and by the rising star, my client, a lowly training officer, one who became increasingly well known and well liked by others in the system, one who was hailed as innovative and personally responsible for the new sense of "empowerment" that permeated employees' attitudes and behaviors in both the HRD department and in other departments once the trainees returned from the program.

We didn't pay attention to the simple fact that this "empowerment stuff" is so potent that it can only be tolerated in a system if everyone in the system is healthy enough to allow it to flourish. It appears that when the HRD manager was asked to provide "something for the lower level folks who have been asking for some training," he was willing to authorize a project which he thought would make him look "progressive" and in touch with the system's needs.

He didn't expect much, and didn't care enough about what we were doing to become a part of what was happening. Throughout the 18-month period that this program was alive, he never visited the training site, even after the president of the airline and others began to rave about the results.

We misinterpreted his neglect as approval, his lack of interest we saw as curious rather than ominous, and we took comfort in believing that the benefits to the system would surely outweigh any concerns that he might have about who was receiving credit for the changes that were occurring in his department. After all, the changes were all positive, weren't they?

Wrong! When the HRD manager finally took action, it was to try to gain control over the project by insisting on changes in personnel, format, etc. This rational was that he could "improve" what had been started and that, as my client's boss, he could make whatever changes he wanted to. We saw this as the act of a desperate man who felt his credibility and authority were under attack.

It bears repeating. Empowerment and encouragement are potent catalysts for change. While many *say* they support these values, they many not be able to support the changes in attitude and behavior that follow when employees begin to act on them.

In our sad tale, one man was able to squash a promising program that was beginning to affect a whole system. Once he killed the program, saving face for himself was given a higher priority than preserving the program, and the system returned to "normal." My client quit, as expected, and I lost out on a wonderful project.

In our excitement (and with our good intentions as our only focus once we got rolling) what we forgot to remember was that "empowerment" efforts and changes always occur within a larger context; all factors need to be constantly monitored. The pacing of our strategies for these changes needs to be appropriate to the larger context, and this too needs to be monitored and adjusted so that support is maintained for the long term.

Authors' Comment

This is a good example of "winning the battle but losing the war!" Obviously, it is our intention to encourage the process of empowered leadership. However, change in and of itself can be viewed negatively, even if the innovation is useful. Encouragement must be an upward, downward, and lateral process. In the above case study, both the consultant and her client misread the lack of involvement as approval as the project progressed. Remember, *the encouragement process does not take place in a vacuum.* A systems approach is essential.

The case study also illustrates the leadership challenge that many middle managers feel. Many middle managers feel like they have all the responsibility and none of the authority and often feel "squeezed" between their boss and their subordinates. In addition to the challenge of effectively motivating one's workers, it is also important to maintain a satisfactory relationship with one's boss. "Buttering up" the boss is not what encouragement means; that is more like manipulation. The stronger the boss's ego, the more likely he or she is to appreciate and value success.

Too much success can be viewed as a threat by insecure leaders who demand that all success be attributed to them. This is one reason for the rise in the number of entrepreneurs, which is discussed in the next chapter. Some people "outshine" or "outgrow" their boss; nonetheless, it is wise to remember that CEOs and top management need encouragement. Involving as many levels of the organization as possible maximizes the likelihood that the initial success will be ongoing.

This poignant case study also helps illustrate that successful leadership often comes with a negative emotional "price tag." Sometimes there are "costs" to being a leader. The phrase "it's lonely at the top" vividly illustrates that leaders must have the courage to make what may be unpopular decisions. Leaders can be so dependent upon the approval of others that they do not have the inner self-encouraging resources to act on their convictions. While it does not appear that the approval of the boss was a key motivator in the above situation, the "cost" of not having the support of the boss was that the program was eventually terminated not *despite* its success but *because* of it.

Often, courageous leadership is at the expense of popularity. For example, President Harry Truman's controversial decision to drop two atomic bombs on Japan is still being debated decades later.

The paradox of leadership by encouragement is that it needs to extend to horizontal and vertical aspects of an organization. At the same time, encouragement also needs to be an *internal* self-oriented approach. A person who is easily swayed by a desire for praise or the approval of others may lack the necessary internal strength of character, the inner "existential anchor" that holds a ship safely despite the "storms" of criticism and disapproval. Finding inner strength and guidance, or *self-encouragement,* is thus a major point of this book.

While most of the examples presented will be *interpersonal* ones, between two or more people, it is also important to have an *internal* self-encouragement program. In fact, psychologist Abraham Maslow suggested that two-thirds of what we characterize as "encouragement strokes" needs to be *internal* in origin, with the remaining one-third coming from others.

Encouraging leadership sometimes means disagreeing with the boss. Again, first-rate leaders hire first-rate followers. Encouragement is *not* obedience or conformity. This was poignantly illustrated in *Gettysburg,* a powerful movie about the Civil War battle. The Northern troops were spread in a long but thin perimeter line. Southern General Robert E. Lee decided to concentrate his troops at the very center of the line, believing it was most vulnerable there. As he discussed his strategy with his various commanders, one was adamantly opposed to the plan. He contended that the charge would be in a half-mile of open field where the superior artillery fire of the Union troops would prevail. He estimated an 80 percent casualty rate just in reaching the opposition. Once there, the Southern soldiers would have to scale a barbed-wire fence, making them easy prey for the rifle fire. Thus, another 80 percent casualty rate was predicted at this obstacle. Despite these concerns, General Lee made what proved to be a costly error by proceeding with an ill-fated charge which indeed turned out just as his wise commander had predicted. After the devastating loss of the majority of his troops, including an entire division of soldiers, General Lee lamented his decision with the commander. "I simply thought we were invincible," Lee confided.

"Groupthink" is a group dynamics phenomenon which has been used to describe President John F. Kennedy's misguided "Bay of Pigs" invasion of Cuba. After the disastrous defeat of the U.S. troops, members of the President's Security Council were interviewed regarding their unanimous endorsement of the invasion. Most members admitted that they had reservations about the proposal but also felt that the "powerful" United States would be invincible against "helpless" Cuba. Because many had recently been appointed to the council, they felt that sharing their concerns would spoil the team spirit of the Security Council. Thus, they withheld their personal reservations in team deliberations.

Former General Motors CEO Roger Smith is credited with the following first-rate leadership decision. The company was considering an acquisition of another financially troubled manufacturer. "Can you think of any reason why we should *not* make this acquisition?" Smith asked his executive vice presidents. Not a single objection was voiced as each executive nodded "no" to the question. "Neither can I think of any objections," Smith noted after polling his team members. "Therefore I suggest that maybe we haven't thoroughly explored the situation," he surprisingly concluded. "I suggest we take another month to see if we have not in fact overlooked something." The group indeed discovered several negative factors and actually voted down the proposed acquisition one month later.

Thus, leadership by encouragement is not blind obedience or conformity. Encouragement is not just an "everything is great, we are wonderful, we can do anything, rah, rah, rah" philosophy. To encourage sometimes means being honest with one's boss even if it may be unpopular.

This case also illustrates that even the "right" empowering leadership strategies can have negative consequences. This is sometimes the emotional "cost" of leadership by encouragement. Being a leader can be lonely and frightening. However, a good antidote for such feelings is *courage,* the topic of our next section.

COURAGE

Another core component of the psychology of encouragement is courage. *Webster's Dictionary* defines courage as "mental or moral strength to venture, persevere, and withstand danger, fear, or difficulty." A major barrier in developing courage is fear, the emotion that contrasts with courage.

Courage and Fears: The Paradox

"**O**ne man with courage makes a majority."

Andrew Jackson

One specific technique that psychologists employ to help individuals change from a fearful to a courageous approach is the use of paradox. Positive growth often occurs when a person can be encouraged to do the very thing he or she fears. Acting as if one has the courage to confront one's concerns is a paradoxical power strategy that often improves self-confidence. For example, an employee who fears making a presentation at the monthly staff meeting could be invited to act as if he or she had the necessary ability to speak clearly and forcefully.

Examples of Courage

The following are some examples of courage. You are invited to add your own personal illustrations to the list. The "total person" has the courage to:

1. Take responsibility for his or her own life rather than blame others for personal problems

2. Be imperfect

3. Say no and mean it

4. Take a risk by engaging in new behaviors

5. Experience intimate, loving relationships

6. Recognize that the healthy personality integrates both masculine and feminine characteristics

7. Live fully in the here and now rather than feel guilty about the past or worry about the future

8. Stand up for his or her personal beliefs

9. Be still and experience the "inner guiding light"

Courage in Action

"I'd rather see a sermon than hear one any day" is exemplified by two modern examples of living courage. The lives of the following two men were congruent with the concept of courage.

> "To be courageous requires no exceptional qualifications, no magic formula, no special combination of time, place, and circumstances. It is an opportunity that sooner or later is presented to us all. In whatever area of life one may meet the challenge of courage, whatever may be the sacrifices he faces if he follows his conscience—the loss of his friends, his fortune, his contentment, even the esteem of his fellow men—each man must decide for himself the course he will follow. The stories of past courage can define that ingredient. They can teach; they can offer hope; they can provide inspiration. But they cannot supply courage itself. For this each man must look into his own soul."
>
> John F. Kennedy

> "We must constantly build dikes of courage
> to hold back the flood of fear."
>
> Martin Luther King, Jr.

Encouragement is more than a philosophy. It involves a set of skills that are described throughout this book. The skills, which are also set forth in *The Skills of Encouragement,* include:

*   Getting high on yourself
*   Listening to build relationships
*   Responding with understanding
*   Building agreement to create a bond

- Believing to communicate your respect
- Enthusiasm to create energy
- Focusing on assets, strengths, and resources
- Perceptual alternatives
- Humor to lighten things up
- Recognizing discouraging beliefs
- Focusing on effort
- Rational thinking to defeat discouragement
- Goal commitment to define your destination
- Optimism to find the best vantage point
- Positive leadership
- Self-encouragement[10]

The psychology of encouragement is founded on a philosophy of courage and hope.

ACTIVITIES

Examples of Encouraging and Discouraging Leaders

To understand the psychology of encouragement, identify some of the most *discouraging* leaders you have ever encountered. They could be teachers, coaches, former or current bosses, or even your parents. First record some of your general *feelings* about these people.

I felt _____

_____

Now identify specific *behaviors* they exhibited.

They would _____

_____

Next, consider the most *encouraging* leaders you have ever encountered. What do you experience when you remember them?

I feel _____

_____

What specific *behaviors* did they exhibit?

They _____

_____

You as an Encouraging Leader: A Self-Assessment

Lucy to Charlie Brown:

> "**Y**ou, Charlie Brown, are in the shadow of your own goal post; you are three putts on the 18th green, you are a seven-ten split in the 10th frame; you are a missed freethrow; a love set; you have dropped a rod and reel in the lake of life; a shanked iron; a third strike; you, Charlie Brown, are a foul ball in the line drive of life!"
>
> Charles Schultz

In *The Motivating Team Leader*, Lewis Losoncy charts 28 distinguishing characteristics of encouraging and discouraging leaders. Some of these characteristics have been adapted in the form of self-appraisal questions.[11]

Respond to the following statements by rating each statement in terms of your own leadership style, as follows:

A = This statement is definitely (strongly) characteristic of me.

B = This statement is somewhat characteristic of me.

C = This statement is probably not characteristic of me.

D = This statement is definitely not characteristic of me.

_____ 1. I spend a great deal of time listening to my people.

_____ 2. I have been spending more time fixing what my people do incorrectly.

_____ 3. My people rarely have new ideas.

_____ 4. My people trust me.

_____ 5. I only recognize jobs well done.

_____ 6. I have a talent scout's ability to see hidden assets and re-sources in my people.

_____ 7. I take on too much, including what should be other people's responsibilities.

_____ 8. I have created an atmosphere in which people can laugh at mistakes.

_____ 9. My people see me as a perfectionist.

_____ 10. I am a team player, and everyone has his or her responsibilities.

Total your score as follows. For items 1, 4, 6, 8, and 10, give yourself 4 points for every A, 3 points for every B, 2 points for every C, and 1 point for every D. For items 2, 3, 5, 7, and 9, give yourself 4 points for every D, 3 points for every C, 2 points for every B, and 1 point for every A.

Now total your points. A score between 30 and 40 denotes a highly encouraging leader. A score between 20 and 29 denotes an above-average encouraging leader. A score of 19 or below denotes a discouraging leader.

Next, list an example for each characteristic that follows.

1. I spend a great deal of time listening to my people.
   Example:

2. I have been spending more time fixing what my people do incorrectly.
   Example:

3. My people rarely have new ideas.
   Example:

4. My people trust me.
   Example:

5. I only recognize jobs well done.
   Example:

6. I have a talent scout's ability to see hidden assets and resources in my people.
   Example:

7. I take on too much, including what should be other people's responsibilities.
   Example:

8. I have created an atmosphere in which people can laugh at mistakes.
   Example:

9. My people see me as a perfectionist.
   Example:

10. I am a team player, and everyone has his or her responsibilities.
    Example:

Summarize your own leadership strengths and weaknesses here:

Your Leadership Style: An Invitation

The best leaders bring about results without making those who are doing the work realize that they are being influenced.

In addition to your self-assessment, you are now invited to have the courage to seek some comparative data from the actual recipients of your leadership—your employees. Use clean copies of the preceding question-naire. You may want to select two extremes, your best worker and your most challenging worker, or you may want to distribute the questionnaire anonymously. Encourage workers to rate you or to cite specific examples just as you did.

Once you have tabulated your scores on their feedback, complete the following.

1. Comparing my own scores to my workers' scores revealed that

2. My reactions and feelings are

3. I expected

4. I was surprised that

5. These areas are my greatest assets as a leader:

6. These areas are my greatest challenges and blind spots as a leader:

7. Specifically, my next steps in encouraging myself to be a more effective leader are

KEY POINTS

1. Leadership by encouragement is a fundamental principle, a corner-stone on which a more humane workplace can be established.

2. Encouragement is the process of facilitating the development of an individual's inner resources and courage toward positive movement from an "I can't" to an "I will" position.

3. An optimistic, encouraged, "the glass is half full" philosophy has a strong correlation with an encouraging approach, in contrast to a pessimistic, discouraged, "the glass is half empty" attitude.

4. Martin Seligman has identified three specific attributes of optimism: performance, pervasiveness, and personalization.

5. Stephen Covey identifies "abundance managers" as having an internal source of identity, seeking solitude and enjoying nature, "sharpening the saw" through continual mental and physical renewal, serving others anonymously, maintaining long-term intimate relationships, forgiving themselves and others, and problem solving rather than blaming.

6. One way of disputing negative self-evaluations and self-criticisms is the ABCDE model developed by Albert Ellis and Martin Seligman, where A = activating events or adversity, B = beliefs, C = consequence or feelings, D = disputation, and E = energization.

7. An encouraging attitude is based on courage and hope.

LEADERSHIP BY ENCOURAGEMENT APPLICATIONS

1. Identify two or three areas of leadership where you personally feel discouraged. Prior to encouraging your employees, take the initial steps toward encouraging *yourself* first. Specifically identify your own discouragement. See if you can *reframe* your own beliefs by disputing possible irrational ideas.

2. Earlier in the chapter, you identified characteristics of your own encouraging leaders. Review your list again. How have you incorporated those characteristics into your own leadership philosophy and style? Create an action plan to further develop those positive attributes in yourself.

3. Begin to keep a personal encouragement journal. React to the content of each chapter. With which points are you in agreement? In disagreement? Cite personal examples that illustrate the theory in action. Then write your own personal commitment to being more

encouraging. Cite specific examples where you feel you have discouraged your workers. Contemplate how encouraging yourself must precede encouraging them.

4. Review the seven characteristics of abundance managers as defined by Covey. Rate yourself from 1 to 10 (1 = lowest, 10 = highest) on each characteristic. Then write a brief explanation of what each number means to you. Finally, list the specific changes you believe are necessary to improve your own ratings.

ENCOURAGEMENT SKILLS

1. Awareness of one's behavior and attitude is a necessary first step toward becoming a more encouraging leader. Begin the process of self-reflection, self-encouragement, and self-confrontation by focusing on your language. There is a verbal skill involved in encouragement. For one week, simply record how many times you say "I (or you) *can't...*," "I (or you) *won't...*," "It is *impossible* to...," and similar statements. Note the specific situations or circumstances in which such comments are made.

2. Step two is to couple the awareness of using such discouraging language with replacing it by saying "I (or you) *chose* not to...," "*Up until now*...has been a challenging situation," etc. The specific skill being addressed involves awareness coupled with an actual change in language that reflects a willingness to modify the underlying belief from which such statements are derived. A related skill involves the reframing or reinterpretation of fatalistic statements to allow creativity to be part of a problem-solving orientation.

3. Self-encouragement and self-confrontation are interdependent skills. Focus on your hopes and fears for this book by:

   A. *Encouraging yourself.* What strengths/assets do you feel currently lead you to being an encouraging leader? What skills do you feel you need to develop to improve yourself as a leader?

   B. *Confronting yourself.* Identify some of the ways you can sabotage or resist any of the ideas and concepts presented in this book (e.g., "What do *they* know about being a manager?" or "It's all just theory").

REFERENCES

1. Kern, R., Leadership, group dynamics, and organizational effectiveness workshop presented in Ottawa, Canada, July 25–August 5, 1994.

2. Dinkmeyer, D. and Losoncy, L., *The Encouragement Book: Becoming a Positive Person,* New York: Prentice-Hall, 1980, p. 65.

3. Dreikurs, R., *Social Equality, The Challenge for Today,* Chicago: Henry Regnery, 1971.

4. Jampolsky, G., *Love Is Letting Go of Fear,* Berkeley, CA: Celestial Arts, 1979.

5. Rogers, C., *Carl Rogers on Personal Power,* New York: Delacorte, 1977.

6. Seligman, M., *Learned Optimism,* New York: Simon & Schuster, 1992.

7. Ellis, A., *Reason and Emotion in Psychotherapy,* New York: Stuart, 1979.

8. Levine, S. and Crom, M., *The Leader in You,* New York: Simon & Schuster, 1993.

9. Covey, S.R., *Principle-Centered Leadership,* New York: Simon and Schuster, 1992.

10. Dinkmeyer, D. and Losoncy, L., *The Skills of Encouragement,* Delray Beach, FL: St. Lucie Press, 1995.

11. Losoncy, L., *The Motivating Team Leader,* New York: Prentice-Hall, 1985.

2

A PHILOSOPHY OF LEADERSHIP

"The way management treats the associates is
exactly how the associates will then treat the customers."

Sam Walton

INTRODUCTION

An essential ingredient of leadership by encouragement is truly valuing
and respecting workers. The philosophy of the encouraging leader is
integrated with the psychology of leadership. The following characteristics
of both the philosophy and the psychology of leadership provide an
overview of the orientation of the encouraging leader.

The Philosophy of Encouragement

1. People are the most underdeveloped resource of the organization.
   Encouraged people have self-esteem, are cooperative, and want to
   be productive.

2. Productivity is increased by soliciting and using the ideas of workers at every level. This must be done systematically.

3. The effective leader is a facilitator who creates situations in which employees can grow, contribute, and produce.

4. Excellence comes from clear goals, decisions made by open discussion so all are participating fully, and decisive actions. Each person is fully responsible for his or her actions and results.

5. People are motivated by their goals and by a feeling of belonging. As you align personal goals with organizational goals and create a community of acceptance and belonging, destructive tension is reduced and productivity is increased.

The Psychology of Encouragement

1. We choose, decide, and act in terms of our goals and purposes. Goals are the final explanations for all behavior.

2. Belonging is a basic need of the individual and is necessary to stimulate organizational growth.

3. People seek to move from less significance to positions in which they are recognized and valued.

4. Behavior is a result of the perception or meaning we give to our experiences.

5. Discouraged people lack self-esteem and a desire to cooperate. They believe that they cannot be successful by contributing, so they resort to passive, destructive ways of relating. They doubt their abilities. They are characterized by a focus on external control and evaluation, unrealistic standards, and emphasis on personal gain.

6. Encouragement identifies the positive potential in every situation.

7. Encouragement provides recognition through the power of positive feedback.

8. Encouraging leaders move from power over others to empowering others.

A Management Systems, Inc. survey of 10,000 workers found that nearly half thought they could be at least 15 percent more productive if management were more responsive to their needs.[1]

Workplace trauma is a more crippling and devastating problem for employees and employers alike than all other work-related stresses combined. Workplace trauma is defined as the disintegration of an employee's fundamental self, which results from an employer or supervisor's perceived or real continual malicious treatment. Job pressures have been cited in 75 percent of claims for worker's compensation in which mental stressors were the main causes of absenteeism. Court decisions affirm that the creation of a work environment that may be perceived as offensive, threatening, or hostile is sufficient basis for liability on the part of the employer.

The growing responsibility to provide a humane workplace is more than a legal one. The economic downturn, along with increasing cost-consciousness, is creating new challenges in motivating employees for peak performance. Although pay raises and bonuses may have been viewed as strong incentives, it is the feelings of accomplishment, recognition, or advancement that truly motivate people. These rewarding feelings are the benefits of the encouraging leader.[2]

In this chapter, a case study is presented to illustrate the interrelationship of technical and psychological issues in organizations. Following the case study, an overview of some key leadership trends establishes the context for a discussion of specific aspects of leadership by encouragement.

CASE STUDY: THE BEGINNING ENTREPRENEUR

"Whenever you see a successful business,
someone once made a courageous decision."

Peter Drucker

When asked, "Who do you work for?" more and more people respond proudly by saying, "I work for myself!" The American frontier encourages entrepreneurs to stake a claim for themselves. It has been said that, "To be a successful entrepreneur, you have to do exactly what people tell you not to do. Being totally crazy and not listening in the end pays off."[3]

Research on more than 200 thriving ventures reveals several helpful guidelines for aspiring founders. First, effective entrepreneurs screen out unpromising ideas as early as possible, and they accomplish this through judgment and reflection as opposed to gathering lots of data. Next, they assess realistically their financial situation, personal preferences, and goals for the venture. In this way, they gauge the attractiveness of an idea and choose just the right new enterprise. Surviving the inevitable disappointments on the rough road to success requires a passion for the business.

"**Y**ou miss 100 percent of the shots you never take."

Wayne Gretzky

To conserve time and money, successful new founders also minimize the resources they devote to researching ideas. The appropriate analytical priorities will vary for each venture. Unlike managers in big corporations, entrepreneurs do not need all the answers to act. In fact, analyzing and acting are difficult to separate in entrepreneurial environments. Smart founders dive in and improvise, and as soon as problems arise, they begin looking for solutions. They plug holes quickly and change strategies as events unfold. Entrepreneurs typically lack the time and money to interview a representative cross section of potential customers, let alone analyze substitutes, reconstruct competitors' cost structures, or project an alternative technology scenario.[4]

Three personality characteristics have received considerable attention in the research: (1) personal values such as honesty, duty, responsibility, and ethical behavior; (2) risk-taking propensity; and (3) the need for achievement.

Forbes magazine interviewed 50 founders from a list of 200 best small companies. In talking with this immensely disparate group, virtually all of the founders said that if their business had gone under, they would definitely have started another. Some call it the "spider syndrome."

Wharton's Edward Moldt has identified a few general traits that most successful entrepreneurs seem to share:

- *Self-confidence*—The ability to overcome fear of failure and inspire confidence in customers, investors, and associates

- *Persistence*—Remaining inwardly optimistic and not being shattered by frequent turndowns

- *Resilience*—The inner strength that enabled Robert the Bruce to roar back after suffering frequent defeats

- *Independence*—Getting satisfaction from being responsible to oneself and not to superiors

- *Daring*—This is not gambling but coolly evaluating risk and not being afraid of it[5]

Case Study

The following case study describes the efforts of one individual in establishing his own company. It is presented to introduce various issues in addition to the "people problems" that challenge a fledgling organization.

For 15 years, John Quincy sold fabrics for a large retail company. He enjoyed the work, the customers, and the manager, but not the pay. He quietly yearned to have his own business. He heard a speaker at a business conference say that every business is based on a need—on a problem waiting to be solved. His wife listened to a review of the speech and then asked him, "What problems do you see in the fabrics business?" They discussed many problems he saw in his daily work; he kept coming back to the problem of customer spills on carpets, pillows, draperies, and other fabrics.

The thought haunted him that this might be the problem for his business to solve. He knew nothing about chemistry but began to experiment at home with liquids to remove stains. Neither he nor his customers were satisfied with products on the market, so he developed new substances.

After six discouraging months, he realized that he still could not remove fabric stains effectively. One day, Mrs. Quincy asked him why he didn't try to prevent stains rather than remove them. The idea sent him into a frenzy of new thinking. He began developing stain-resistant liquids to cover new fabrics. Soon he perfected one, then three, then five liquids that coated various surfaces to prevent stains from setting.

He wisely kept his retail job until he had the products patented and their names copyrighted. At home, he mixed the chemicals, packaged the products, and worked on advertising. After much experimental application of his products, he began to make barrels of the five chemical mixtures in his basement. After securing his first sizable sale to a fabric retailer, he believed he could make it on his own. He mustered his courage and took the big risk of resigning from his retail job to work full-time on his new products.

He borrowed money, rented space, and began working day and night, performing every function of the business. He bought, mixed, and bottled the chemicals; he did the selling; and he handled the legal aspects, accounting, banking, correspondence, packaging, shipping, billing, cleaning, and delivery. He also invented.

The business grew more rapidly than expected and became large enough that Quincy needed help. First he hired a mechanical person with a knowledge of chemistry to mix the liquids and to handle maintenance. As sales accelerated, he hired an experienced office manager as secretary/bookkeeper/receptionist, who proved to be decisive and responsible.

Quincy faced his first people-management problem when his office manager began to resent his wife's frequent visits to the office. A power struggle developed when Mrs. Quincy defined and delineated specific job responsibilities in a written job description for both employees, who were women. At home, she criticized the office manager, making it difficult for her husband to balance the complaints and contributions of both employees.

During the second year, Mr. Quincy hired seven production workers and one more office person; a strong leader who was acceptable to everyone emerged as a foreman. The following year, Quincy hired a sales/general manager. Profits were good, but this new person turned out to be overambitious, competitive with Quincy, and dishonest. Mr. Quincy had trusted him and had not kept an eye on his activities; thus, he almost lost his business because of the man's unethical dealings with patent attorneys and customers.

The first outside experts Quincy sought were a personnel consultant, a banker, and a public accountant. The personnel consultant helped to create recruiting and hiring policies that were legally and psychologically sound; wrote functional job descriptions; established orientation procedures; formulated motivational pay systems; developed insurance, medical service, and attendance records; began training programs at all levels; and established a communications system throughout the company. The banker advised Quincy on seasonal financing and reinvesting. The public accountant helped him keep appropriate records and books for the shop, for the office, and for his own tax accounting.

Quincy was forced from the start to consider the people aspects of manufacturing management as well as the need for awareness of every department. As the number of employees grew, the most challenging part of his business seemed to be the people aspect. When he walked through the plant one day during the third year, he discovered that he did not know everyone's name. A night janitor asked him what he was doing in the shop. The new receptionist refused to let his wife interrupt him in a meeting. As the company grew, impersonality became a problem, as people knew less and less about one another. He learned that each person he hired wanted to get to know him, but he had trouble keeping in touch with employees and he worried about loyalty and morale as well as productivity and profitability.

The case history of Mr. Quincy is a composite story of several of the authors' actual consulting clients. It has been selected to focus on the growing number of small-business entrepreneurs. It demonstrates that human interactions and relationships are a major challenge for business leaders. In *Megatrends 2000,* Naisbitt and Aburdene make the following prediction: "The primary challenge of leadership in the 1990s is to encourage the new, better-educated worker to be more entrepreneurial, self-managing, and oriented toward lifelong learning."[6]

The rapid expansion of high technology increases rather than decreases the "people" portion of the successful business equation. The phrase "high tech–high touch" was introduced by Naisbitt in *Megatrends* to denote the vital importance of both the technical and the human relationship polarities. "Whenever new technology is introduced into society, there must be a counterbalancing human response—that is, 'high touch'—or the technology is rejected. The more high tech, the more high touch." Naisbitt later urges, "We must learn to balance the material wonders of technology with the spiritual demands of our human nature."[7]

People are the most important and least developed resource of an organization. Companies that spend millions on new product development, machinery, and advertising often are remiss in providing a budget to train their people. The encouraging leader is the "high touch" human component that is increasingly important in an increasingly technical work world.

CHARACTERISTICS OF ENTREPRENEURS

Economists and business experts agree that entrepreneurs are the Lewis and Clarks of today's business world. Blazing new business trails, they risk their savings, their time, and their security to follow a dream product, service, or idea. And they often fail within the first year. Yet the successful ones, along with their small business cousins, account for more than two-thirds of the new jobs created in the United States.

Entrepreneurs need vision and the ability to operate independently. They need confidence. They need the ability to marshal their resources and lead people to buy their products.

It is also a rule of thumb that the entrepreneur cannot afford to get hung up on status. The one-person show is more the rule than the exception, and the entrepreneur can expect to do it all—including clerical and janitorial work—at some point.[8]

According to Miles Hardy, "An entrepreneur is like a football coach who gambles on fourth down. If the play fails, the crowd boos. If it succeeds, the coach is a hero."

"The entrepreneur is usually described as someone who is exploitive, tends to be aggressive, tends to take advantage of the situation," notes Hardy. "These are traits not usually found in the people that we like best. If he's successful, we think 'What a chancy, risky guy,' but if he fails, we think he's a sociopath."[8]

An entrepreneur is often a leader who relies on people to accomplish purposes and objectives. The leadership school of entrepreneurship is a non-technical side of the management school which suggests that entrepreneurs need to be skilled in appealing to others to "join the cause." A successful entrepreneur must also be a people manager or an effective leader/mentor who plays a major role in motivating, directing, and leading people. "Thus, the entrepreneur must be a leader, able to define a vision of what is possible, and attract people to rally around that vision and transform it into reality."[9]

An important aspect of leadership is how a leader gets tasks accomplished and responds to the needs of people. Two dimensions are important for the management of an enterprise—a concern for getting the task accomplished and a concern for the people doing the work.[10]

The late Richard Buskirk was professor of marketing and director of the entrepreneur program at the University of Southern California. His classic work *The Entrepreneur's Handbook*[11] is an excellent resource for the journey toward becoming an entrepreneur. He isolated 13 specific entrepreneurial traits which he feels characterize successful leaders by contrasting them with what he calls a "bureaucratic mentality." In a series of public talks in Oita City and Tokyo, Japan in November 1993, he contrasted the entrepreneurial and the bureaucratic business approaches in the following 13 ways.

1. Attitude toward failure—Many people will not start a new business because they are afraid they will fail. To them, few things are worse than failing, worse than making a mistake. "Better not to try than to fail" is the bureaucrat's response to our culture's emphasis on success, or at least the appearance of success.

Entrepreneurs believe they can handle whatever problems arise. Somehow, they will prevail. They will win. Thus, failure is not something that they unduly fear. In fact, many entrepreneurs have said that they used whatever fear of failure they had as a tool, as a force to make them work even harder to avoid it.

Moreover, if they fail, they consider it a lesson learned. They look upon their early failures as the hot coals that forged their ultimate success. As the saying goes, "Show me someone who has not failed and I'll show you someone who has not tried."

2. *Results oriented*—Now let's talk about results—sales and profits. Call it profit orientation, or what you will, but entrepreneurs are interested in results. On the other hand, bureaucrats are largely interested in process as opposed to the results of the process. The corporate bureaucrat is so concerned with company procedures and processes that she or he loses sight of the end results. Are the costs of the procedures warranted by the resulting profits? Are the costs effective? As long as the bureaucrat meets budgets, all is well.

3. *Acceptance of responsibility*—Entrepreneurs take responsibility for what happens, good or bad. This is one of the key aspects of owning a business. *You* are the boss, and the boss is responsible for what happens.

It is important for the bureaucrat to avoid responsibility and, therefore, blame. Bureaucrats appoint committees, hire consultants, do research, or whatever else is necessary to make certain the responsibility for everything is well-diffused and transferred elsewhere.

4. *Willingness to sacrifice.* Entrepreneurs want to win. Some want to win so badly that they sometimes do things that perhaps they should not, but such is the nature of the highly competitive person.

On the other hand, bureaucrats often play for the tie. In the literature, this is called a zero sum game, where no one wins. Some people blame the U.S. defeats in Korea and Vietnam on Washington bureaucrats who did not want to win. They wanted a stalemate, a tie. There is a price for winning, and if you are not willing to pay it, you are likely to lose. Entrepreneurs are willing to pay the price. Bureaucrats are not.

5. *Action oriented*—The entrepreneur seeks action and wants to make things happen. The bureaucrat avoids action because it entails risk and work, two things to be avoided to the bureaucratic mind.

True, the entrepreneur often seeks too much action, action for its own sake, or action to counter boredom. This is a tendency entrepreneurs must control, but, on balance, it is more desirable than the inactivity of the bureaucrat.

The American government is currently in gridlock. Bureaucrats seem to do nothing more than disagree and blame each other, things they are very good at doing. This orientation is related to winning, but you usually cannot win without some action. Two key words for the would-be entrepreneur are *do it*. Get into action! Make something happen! Often the only difference between the successful entrepreneur and someone who works for a large organization is that the entrepreneur had the courage to take action. We call this initiative.

6. Sensitivity to opportunity—Entrepreneurs look for opportunities that they may be able to turn to their advantage. They are opportunity conscious. Fortunes have resulted from such vigilance.

To the bureaucrat, an opportunity is just another chance to fail. To see an opportunity and fail to act upon it is a social stigma. Thus, the adept, well-trained bureaucrat has learned not to recognize opportunities. Better yet, he or she has learned to translate opportunity into other things.

7. Market oriented—The entrepreneur knows that all business starts with the customer. Customers are the source of all the good things you want to happen. A repeat customer is an annuity—an asset that will pay you money on and on into the future as long as you take good care of it. Thus, the care and feeding of customers should be foremost in the minds of most entrepreneurs.

How many bureaucrats share such concerns for their customers? Bureaucrats prefer to tell you what you can do. And you pay dearly for their decisions. Big Brother knows what is best for you.

8. Attitude toward constraints—Bureaucrats love constraints. The more, the better. Given enough constraints upon their behavior, they do nothing, a most delightful circumstance to them. Thus, the bureaucrats of the world busy themselves creating constraints for each other—professional courtesy, so to speak. Just look at government constraints on business. The IRS regulations alone greatly constrain business.

Naturally, entrepreneurs hate constraints. They hate the lack of reason in many of the constraints they encounter in undertaking their ventures. Constraints are barriers to action. They keep things from happening.

Of course, some constraints are necessary in any civilized society, and many of them work to the benefit of business. Thus, the person who perpetually battles constraints often self-destructs.

9. Reality perception—Entrepreneurs know that there must be substance and reality to one's enterprise. It cannot be based on dreams, wishful thinking, and high hopes. It must be based on cold hard facts (i.e., actual costs, real sales, real markets).

On the other hand, bureaucrats are occupied with appearances—the appearance of importance, the appearance of being busy, the appearance of power. They are concerned about being politically correct in their speech and behavior, while doing their best to avoid the reality of the situation.

10. Leadership tactics—The entrepreneur leads by personal contract and example. One of the virtues of working for a smaller enterprise is that the boss deals directly with the employees, often on a first-name basis.

In contrast, the memo is the favorite communication tool of bureaucrats. They love to put things in writing—memos, reports, letters, forms, etc. This allows them to avoid facing someone and thus exposing themselves to cross examination on whatever information is being communicated. Paper can hide much incompetence. It can also expose it if you know how to read the paper.

Naturally, paper is necessary in our society. Talk is elusive and subject to distortion. Thus, the adept entrepreneur must learn the paper game for self-protection.

11. Dislike of staff operations—Entrepreneurs favor line operating personnel and prefer to minimize the use of staff personnel in the organization. Indeed, they have great distaste for the staff people they must hire (accountants, whom they often refer to as their bean counters, personnel managers, and the other paper-oriented people in the organization). They cherish salespeople and factory workers. Many entrepreneurs fret over the tendency of staff people who have needed information to assume superiority over line operators. A few talks with salespeople who are fighting with the accounting department outline some of the more common problems.

Bureaucrats, on the other hand, love staff. They are staff. The adept, power-seeking bureaucrat vies with organizational competitors by seeing who can build up the staff. The more people reporting to a bureaucrat, the more power and status he or she has in the organization.

12. Recognition of values—Entrepreneurs value money. They work too hard for it to take it lightly. They treat company money as if it were theirs and therefore use it carefully.

Bureaucrats are not spending their own money, and therefore it has little value to them. Billions of dollars are wasted by bureaucrats. Why not, it isn't their money. Spending other people's money is fun.

13. Career consciousness—Bureaucrats tend to clear all decisions through an automatic screen of "how will this decision affect my career?" They are career conscious. Their first gateway in making a decision is how it will affect them personally. They avoid any threats to their careers. The purchasing agent is not really interested in the best buy for the firm, but instead looks for the "safe" buy. Thus, the large, well-established firm has a huge advantage over the smaller newcomer in selling to such people.

The entrepreneur, on the other hand, does not really have a career, as such. She or he has a business and must think in terms of what is best for that business. The entrepreneurial manager tries to make decisions based on what is best for the company. Entrepreneurs believe they can handle whatever problems arise.

"Today's winners are tomorrow's losers.
We must be developing tomorrow's winners."

Richard Buskirk

EARLY EFFORTS TO HUMANIZE BUSINESS

"In modern organization jargon,
person skills always precede professional skills."

Max DePree

Countless owners of small and large businesses have experienced at least some of the problems described in the case study presented at the start of the chapter. Many imaginative programs to understand and motivate employees have been established. We shall now review some specific innovations.

Frederick Herzberg made significant contributions to the important study of employee motivation by distinguishing what he called "motivators" from "hygiene" factors. He defined motivators as aspects of the job such as achievement, recognition for accomplishment, challenging work, increased responsibility, and growth and development. Conversely, hygiene factors are in the organizational *environment* and include policies and administration, working conditions, interpersonal relations, money, status, and security. Thus, managers need to attend to both motivator and hygiene factors. Leadership by encouragement deals with the important personal factors identified by Herzberg.[12]

The "new" management philosophy, Theory Y, is based on a different understanding of human nature and motivation. Theory Y managers assume that people are basically self-directed and creative at work if properly interested or challenged. Theory Y (encouraging) managers help employees to achieve their goals by directing their efforts toward accomplishing personal and organizational objectives.[13]

William Ouchi presented Theory Z, which is characterized by the Japanese concept of quality circles, or work groups, in which input from all employees is sought and valued. Theory Z is a management style that blends Japanese and American traits to produce organizations that "have it both ways." (Japan contributed long-term employment, consensual decision making, slow promotion and evaluation, and concern for the whole. America contributed informal control, specialized career paths, and individual achievement.) Type Z companies such as Cummins Engine, Delta Airlines, Cray Research, 3M, and Procter & Gamble are known for their high morale, low turnover, and company loyalty.

According to Theory Z, the way to sustain higher levels of production in an affluent society is to assume that the workers have higher needs (for self-esteem, belonging to an organization they can be proud of, realizing their individual potential) and to aim to satisfy those needs by offering responsibility and autonomy at work.[14]

The encouraging leader is based on the philosophy that workers can be self-motivated and self-directed and that higher needs such as self-esteem are better met in an encouraging environment.

Effective leadership addresses both the intellectual and the emotional needs of others. Individuals and social groups need structure and a sense of order for the achievement of goals but, as social animals, also demand to be treated with concern and respect. These two factors are critical to understanding why some leaders are effective while others make the effort but fail. The encouraging leader is based on both a respect for goals and structure and an appreciation of the psychological desire for basic human dignity.

> "Trends, like horses, are easier to ride
> in the direction they are already going."
>
> John Naisbitt

FIVE TRENDS FOR THE MILLENNIUM

As we approach the end of the century, a significant shift in management philosophy is required if organizations are to survive in a changing global economy. The goal of leadership by encouragement is founded on five key trends that characterize effective leadership in this decade:

1. Human capital as a budgeted line item

2. Leadership versus management

3. Leadership in a multicultural world

4. Feminine leadership

5. Both transformational and transactional leadership characterize the "total" leader

Trend 1: Human Capital

The phrase "human capital" has become almost drearily familiar. It entered into common usage among economists 30 years ago, thanks to Gary Becker, a Nobel laureate and professor of economics and sociology at the University of Chicago, who coined it. The term was controversial at first. Many said that it referred to people as slaves or machines. Now, the notion that people and firms invest in skills in much the same way that they invest in plant and machinery (i.e., weighing the costs against the expected returns) seems obvious.

"It's what you learn *after* you know it all that counts."

John Wooden

"Work can provide the opportunity for spiritual and personal, as well as financial, growth. If it doesn't, then we're wasting far too much of our lives on it."

James Autry

Innovations in human capital management are being made in a number of countries. The Swedes have come to understand the importance of healthy workers and the importance of balancing work and family. A recent study of Japanese and American managers found that one distinguishing criterion of the two groups was that the Japanese viewed their employees as assets whereas American managers saw them as costs.[15]

"The inventory goes home at night."

Louis B. Mayer

In a chapter entitled "Untapped Human Capital," Warren Bennis cites the above statement by Louis B. Mayer, former head of MGM Studios. Mayer recognized that it was the people—the directors, writers, and actors—who made MGM a success. Bennis continues: "In the same way, whatever a modern corporation markets, from cars to meals to life insurance, its primary resource is its people. This is a basic economic fact and it is the American business people's refusal to accept and act on it that accounts for America's poor performance in the international marketplace."[16]

Workers have too often been seen in an adversarial light, as mere cogs in the corporate wheel. Dan Eckstein, a former professional athlete, calls it the "NFL syndrome," where someone is always ready to take the place of an injured, aging, or simply unacceptable worker/player. Bennis feels that President Ronald Reagan's decision to fire striking air traffic controllers reinforced the notion that today's workers are anonymous, replaceable, and greedy.

Garfield notes that "reality" is not what it used to be. If the controlling reality in the agricultural age was land and in the industrial age was financial capital, the controlling reality in the information age we have now entered is *human* capital—the ability to use human intelligence and limitless human capacities. Only an outstanding enterprise treats intelligence and human capacity as resources to be actively, consciously cultivated with the same attention given to land and financial capital in the past. Property and money can be manipulated as passive articles. Human capital, however, is a resource that is best invested in and developed with the full, conscious participation of motivated human beings. It is human capital that is building bridges from the industrial age to the information age.[17]

Technical competence is an assumed prerequisite for promotion to a managerial role. Yet too often the skills that lead to technical success do not translate to the needed "people skills." For example, a common practice is to make a unit's top salesperson its leader or to make the best player a coach. However, success as a salesperson or an athlete does not always translate into success as a manager; in fact, it is often detrimental. The high performance standards of the star often create value and inter-personal conflicts. Personal drive for success may be highly valued by an organization when it shows up in the form of long work hours and weekends at the office. What should be given greater value is organiza-tional loyalty from a well-balanced employee who does a good job but chooses to spend personal time with his or her family.

The concept of human capital implies valuing and respecting the psychological needs of all individuals in the organization. The first trend is recognizing that human resource development needs to be valued in organizations. A specific way to do that is to create a budget for people skills.

Dale Carnegie observed that "dealing with people is probably the biggest problem you face...Research...revealed that even in such technical lines as engineering, about 15 percent of one's financial success is due to one's technical knowledge and about 85 percent is due to skill in human engineering—to personality and the ability to lead people."

"There is something that is much more scarce,
something rarer than ability. It is the ability to recognize ability."

Robert Half

Thus, valuing human capital is one key trend in valuing contemporary leadership.

Trend 2: The Shift from Management to Leadership

"**B**eing quality means you contribute much more of what
you have to give than your peers do. You are
a practitioner of authenticity. That's why you stand out."

Allan Cox

There is growing consensus that the 1990s will be considered a leadership
rather than a management era. Naisbitt and Aburdene[6] describe the shift
from management to leadership as follows:

"**T**he dominant principle of organization has shifted from management in order to control enterprise to leadership in order to bring
out the best in people and to respond quickly to change. This is not
the 'leadership' individuals and groups so often call for when they
really want a father figure to take care of all their problems. It is a
democratic yet demanding leadership that respects people and
encourages self-management, autonomous teams, and entrepreneurial units."

Noted business consultants Warren Bennis and Burt Nanus[16] emphasize the difference:

"**B**y focusing attention on a vision, the leader operates on the
emotional and spiritual resources; on its values, commitment, and
aspirations. The manager, by contrast, operates on the physical
resources of the organization, on its capital human skills, raw
materials, and technology...It remains for the effective leader, however, to help people in the organization know pride and satisfaction
in their work...It is an emotional appeal to some of the most
fundamental of human needs—the need to be important, to make
a difference, to feel useful, to be a part of a successful and worthwhile enterprise."

Included in their book *Leaders: The Strategies for Taking Charge* is a
powerful message published by United Technologies Corporation of
Hartford, Connecticut:[16]

"**P**eople don't want to be managed. They want to be led. Whoever
heard of a world manager? World leader, yes. Educational leader.
Political leader. Religious leader. Scout leader. Community leader.
Labor leader. Business leader. They lead. They don't manage....If
you want to manage somebody, manage yourself. Do that well and
you'll be ready to stop managing and start leading."

The distinction between leading and managing is also an important philosophy of total quality proponents.

"**M**anagers control. Leaders create commitment."

John H. Zenger

"**M**anagement is a bottom line focus: How can I best accomplish certain things? Leadership deals with the top line: What are the things I want to accomplish? Management is efficiency in climbing the ladder of success; leadership determines whether the ladder is leaning against the right wall."

Stephen Covey

Thus, a second trend of the 1990s involves a shift from power over people (manager) to shared power, commitment, and vision (leadership).

Trend 3: An Expanded Multicultural and Global Perspective

"**W**hat counts are the things we believe,
our understanding of people, and our embracing of diversity."

Max DePree

The following are key trends of the next decade as predicted by the U.S. Department of Labor. By the year 2000, white males will account for only 15 percent of the 25 million people who join the work force. The remaining 85 percent will consist of white females, immigrants, and minorities (both genders) of black, Hispanic, and Asian origin. It is projected that some time in the next century, non-Hispanic whites will lose their majority status in the United States.

While women will continue to increase as a proportion of the work force (predicted to be 47 percent by the end of the 1990s), the Bureau of Labor Statistics predicts that white males will drop to 39 percent of the labor force by the end of the decade. The number of Asians will be up 80 percent, Hispanics 75 percent, and African-Americans 28 percent. These three microcultures will account for more than 80 percent of the net increase to the work force, comprising 26 percent of the total by the year 2000.[18]

Phillip Harris and Robert Moran have edited a timely "Managing Cultural Series" which consists of several books.* They contrast *assimila-*

---

* Gulf Publishing Company, Box 2608, Houston, TX 77252-2608.

tion with the more preferred concept of *acculturation*. Assimilation is the wholesale rejection of one's own values in order to embrace those of another; conversely, acculturation is learning to talk the language of another culture while remaining firmly rooted in the values and language of one's own. Those who assimilate forfeit their own culture and often with it their own self-esteem. To acculturate one must truly live in two worlds simultaneously, attempting to divide life into separate compartments such as one authority at work and another at home. Twentieth-century leaders will resist the myth of the "melting pot" philosophy of assimilation ("I have to be just like them") and encourage acculturation instead.

> "**W**omen, people of color, white males, new immigrants—none of us actually belongs in a meat grinder or a melting pot. Many cannot, and, today, would not if they could, disappear into a cultural or organizational mainstream. More people than ever are demanding that organizations adapt to cultural differences that they find important. As a manager either you will make it mentally and emotionally clear how everyone can win collaboratively, or else no one will win...
>
> Acculturation is a shared street. Certainly, newcomers to a workplace must learn enough to do their job, become comfortable, and collaborate well within the organization they join. But in the new workplace everyone is a newcomer. The transcultural leader helps the whole organization acculturate to the new workplace culture and become collaborative and productive in it."

In the process of becoming acculturated, Simons, Vazquez, and Harris suggest the following four developmental stages.

1. We enter the new situation with some level of emotional *excitement,* often surprise, caution, or even enthusiasm.

   "I suppose we can get along with these newcomers."

   "Here I am, in the land of opportunity."

   "I'll show everyone how easy it is to work for a woman boss."

2. When the situation turns out to be more challenging than expected, *frustration, anger,* or *depression* is the consequence. Many people stay stuck in this stage.

   "I don't think I'll ever get across to these people."

   "I can't believe she would say a thing like that."

3. We begin a more sober and objective view by *acknowledging real differences* on a practical every day level.

   "We really are different."

   "She and I speak different languages. I'm beginning to see where the misunderstandings occur."

4. Finally, we need to negotiate *workable agreements to collaborate and to produce new results.*

   "We agree to speak English on the job, but we prefer our own language when chatting with each other."

   "We both need to listen very carefully to each other and ask more questions."

They suggest a new version of the 80/20 rule. A business maxim is that 20 percent of the customers account for 80 percent of the sales, or 20 percent of the employees cause 80 percent of a leader's problems. It is suggested that when working with different cultures, the 80/20 rule should be applied in reverse, which means that 80 percent of the breakdown has cultural roots while 20 percent or less is personal. Viewed another way, 20 percent is personal, while 80 percent is systemic, rooted in the structure, values, and rules of the organization itself.[19]

Leadership for the 1990s will involve greater multinational and multicultural awareness and appreciation. Sensitivity to a variety of personal, philosophic, political, and spiritual orientations will characterize the emergent leaders of the next decade.

An awareness and appreciation of the approaches of other cultures to leadership also is essential for the 1990s. According to Japanese businessman Sakan Yanagidaira, leadership by encouragement is similar to an ancient Oriental concept called *kokorozashi*. It originated with Confucius, was later essential to the Samurai, and has recently experienced a resurgence in Japanese leadership philosophy. *Kokorozashi* can be loosely translated as the "leader's mind"—spirited commitments, the intentions, willpower, or primary motivations of a leader. *Kokorozashi* also possesses the energy to create enthusiasm. Unless a leader possesses *kokorozashi,* he or she will not be able to achieve individual or organizational goals, visions, or dreams. To have *kokorozashi* as a leader means to do something for others to better them and to help them motivate themselves through self-encouragement. According to Mr. Yanagidaira, *kokoragashi* is like having better computer software, an improved "thinking" capacity. It is seeing from a higher or broader perspective, including an "upgraded," networking capacity.

During a visit to Japan, Daniel Eckstein asked Mr. Yanagidaira how to contrast American and Japanese management styles. "Tell me how a giraffe and a chimpanzee are different," was Yanagidaira's reply. After listening to a few differences (weight, height, etc.), he said, "Now tell me how they are similar." That required a new cognitive functioning, a restructuring of a predisposition toward finding cultural differences. The wise Japanese CEO then concluded that "most people seek the differences between American and Japanese traditions; I encourage people to seek the similarities instead." Seeking the universality of a global perspective while respecting cultural differences is a trend that will distinguish contemporary leaders.

> "If he works for you, you work for him."
>
> Japanese proverb

The cultural norms that run through Japanese society are unique in many respects. While Westerners may admire these common values, few have examined the leadership norms in Japan in light of that country's values.

Some of the admirable but unduplicated principles that define Japanese society are *amae, anshinkan,* and *kaizen.* Another characteristic is *patient persistence,* typified in the story of Oshin, a poor girl who grew up in poverty in northern Japan. Her perseverance and patience permitted her to overcome hardship and become a successful business executive.

Sweet dependency—*amae*—is the glue that holds Japanese society together. *Amae* is best described as a flexible bonding in a relationship, such as that which occurs between children and parents. The concept is pervasive in Japanese culture, including the corporate world. *Amae* is found in families, the educational environment, and companies that foster dependency, loyalty, a positive image, and a strong work ethic.

Amae in corporate culture in Japan is evident in the worker's pride in his or her company's products and services. The culture is driven by consensus—*anshinkan* (peace of mind)—in workers to help ensure fast implementation of mutually agreed upon organizational goals.

Kaizen, or continuous improvement, drives Japanese workers and managers to focus on the whole process rather than just the end result. Continuous improvement is critical in a country where resources must be used efficiently. An emphasis on efficiency and productivity, which sometimes exists at the expense of harmony, predominates in the manufacturing sector of Japan's economy.[20] Thus, an expanded multicultural perspective characterizes leadership.

Trend 4: Feminine Leadership

Women have gained access to virtually every line of work and are bulging in the management pipeline. Labor Department statistics show that women make up 40 percent of a loosely defined demographic category of executives, administrators, and managers. However, only a very small number of women have top jobs in America's major companies. Although opportunities for women have increased substantially in recent years, a great many barriers still remain, and the unanswered question is why so few women reach senior-level management positions.

In *Success and Betrayal: The Crisis of Women in Corporate America*, Jacobs describes the "BOGSAT" phenomenon—the idea that the most important decisions in organizations are made by a "bunch of guys sitting at a table," which usually means that female employees' concerns are not adequately addressed or championed at the top.[21]

> "**O**ne of the things women do instinctively is praise people.
> That's an important tool.
> Praise doesn't come naturally to the lips of men."
>
> Ann Wexler

One of the most significant trends in the contemporary corporate world is the rapid increase in the number of women managers. For example, in *Megatrends 2000*, one of the top ten forthcoming trends described by Naisbitt and Aburdene is "The 1990s: Decade of Women in Leadership." They report that since World War II, the number of working women has increased 200 percent. In the past 20 years, women have taken two-thirds of the new jobs. Women without children are more likely to work than men (79 percent versus 74 percent), and 67 percent of women with children work. The circulation of *Working Woman* (900,000 copies) surpasses *Fortune, Forbes,* and *Business Week. Working Woman* is the second largest business periodical in publication, exceeded only by the *Wall Street Journal.*

Women are also starting new businesses twice as fast as men. In Canada, one-third of small businesses are owned by women; in France, 20 percent are. Since 1980, the number of self-employed women in Great Britain has increased three times faster than the number of self-employed men. The Small Business Association reports that 30 percent of small businesses are owned by women.

The percentage of women physicians has doubled since 1972, and the number of female lawyers and architects has increased 400 percent. More than one-third of Procter & Gamble and Apple Computer's marketing executives are women. As of 1990, 83 percent of the female officers in Fortune 500 and Service 500 companies held the title of vice president or better, compared with 35 percent in 1980.[21]

Sharon Nelton notes that as of 1990, women owned 5.4 million U.S. businesses and provided employment for nearly 11 million people. A national Women's Business Council was established in 1988 with the enactment of the Women's Business Ownership Act. It currently predicts that by the end of 1992, female-owned firms will surpass the top Fortune 500 firms in providing jobs.[22]

Judy Rosener characterizes female leadership as "interactive" and male leadership as "command-and-control." She further suggests that an interactive (female) leadership style is more effective as the pace of organizational change accelerates in the 1990s. Rosener maintains that interactive leaders are fundamentally different from command-and-control leaders in that they:

1. Encourage participation

2. Share power and information willingly

3. Enhance the self-worth of others[23]

"Everyone has an invisible sign hanging from their neck saying, 'Make me feel important!' Never forget this message when working with people."

Mary Kay Ash

Women leaders often encourage participation and share power and information. Most do not covet formal authority, having learned to lead without it. Sharon Nelton believes that smart companies are making room for diversity by drawing on the complementary leadership styles of both men and women.

Adopting an androgynous management style that balances so-called masculine and feminine traits might help women to overcome the negative effects of sexual stereotyping in the workplace. Thus, they should be perceived by others as both likable and competent.

Household International executive Antonia Shusta believes that too many top male executives downplay the emotional side of life. "Business is all people and people in large degrees are very emotional....If you don't understand emotion, you're missing out on a lot." Shusta believes that because women are better able to cope with the sometimes "messy" emotions of the workplace, they foster a greater sense of belonging in their employees. That, in turn, breeds loyalty and encourages people to do their best.

Leadership studies of the first coed classes at West Point found that male and female cadets performed equally well in getting the job done; however, women were rated higher by their subordinates on looking out for the latter's welfare and showing interest in their lives. Nelton observes that all leadership is becoming more "feminized" simply because it makes good business sense. The result is that in the 1990s, men will be freer to use "feminine" tools of leadership without embarrassment and women will feel freer to use styles more natural to them as individuals.[22]

The encouraging leader stresses that the complete leader is one who can be both masculine and feminine, regardless of his or her sex.

> "From the wall of the middle room, fresh pure water drips constantly. It is as if the walls are weeping; it is as if the soul of contentment is weeping. Why does it weep? It weeps for the decline of poets; it weeps for the bone of the buffalo; it weeps for the black people that think like white people; it weeps for the Indians who think like settlers; it weeps for children who think like adults; it weeps for magic that has been forgotten; it weeps for the free who think like prisoners, but most of all, it weeps for cowgirls who think like cowboys."
>
> Tom Robbins
> *Even Cowgirls Get the Blues*

Trend 5: Both Transformational and Transactional Leadership Characterize the "Total" Leader

In his classic book *Leadership,* James MacGregor Burns distinguished two types of leadership: transformational and transactional. In doing so, Burns recognized that leadership is not a unitary concept, and he used great leaders from history to illustrate this point. Transactional leaders motivate others to believe in desired ways by offering rewards that satisfy the self-interest of followers. There is an exchange of mutually valued things, a transaction between leader and follower, such as higher pay and benefits for higher productivity.

> "The things we fear most in organizations—
> fluctuations, disturbances, imbalances—
> are the primary sources of creativity."
>
> Margaret J. Wheatly

Transformational leaders motivate others to act not out of self-interest but out of commitment to a higher ideal or transcendent goal. Through this relationship, the motivation and maturity of both the leader and the follower are raised to higher levels.

Transformational leaders have been characterized as charismatic, inspirational, able to stimulate others intellectually, and capable of showing individualized consideration. Charisma evokes devotion to and unqualified belief in leaders and their missions. The inspiration of leaders creates a climate of openness and trust. Intellectual stimulation causes followers to see new possibilities and to challenge their own assumptions; individualized consideration focuses on the worth of individuals and their development in the organization. For transformational leaders, the task is one of creation and commitment—creating a vision and then creating new meaning for organization members to secure their commitment to the new vision.[24]

A number of authors assert that leaders typically exhibit both transformational and transactional leadership. Most leaders do both but in different amounts. Both transformational and transactional leadership are necessary, especially in the way we define the terms.

> "The wise administrator does not lead people to set their hearts upon what they cannot have, but satisfies their inner needs."
>
> Lao Tsu

Bernard Bass describes transformational leaders as follows: "They may be *charismatic* to their employees and thus *inspire* them; they may meet the *emotional* needs of each employee; and/or they may intellectually stimulate employees."[25] The leader's vision of what could be is an essential first step in the "total quality" process.

One way to view transformational leadership is in relation to push-and-pull organizational energy. An example of a pushing energy is a mission statement establishing the specific business in which the organization is involved. Strategic planning and the yearly budget process are examples of other organizational tools which organize, synthesize, reward, and inform.

Conversely, pull tools create a future state toward which people can be drawn. Creating a common organizational vision is an example. Whereas push tools set parameters and limits, pull tools enable people to establish their own boundaries. Push tools are often imposed by a small number of other people (usually bosses), whereas pull tools allow people to motivate themselves from within. Pull tools help with the creation of a common, concrete vision and a visualized picture of the future that is inspiring, shared, and consistent among employers. Both push and pull energies are needed.

Transformational leaders can use the analogy of a skyscraper consisting of three segments to help establish an effective vision. Segment I consists of *values* ("What do I believe in and what has meaning to me?"). Segment 2 consists of the most vital or "A-list" items ("How will I know? What do I want? Why do I want it?"). Segment 3 includes specific *descriptions* of how the company will be in the future ("What will I feel?" "What will I hear?" "What will I see?").[26]

> "Nothing happens unless first a dream."
>
> Carl Sandburg

A second essential leadership style is the *transactional* leader. Transactional leaders are often more subtle and less visible than transformational leaders, who have the ability to actively shape or change the direction of a group due to their visionary capacities. Transactional and transformational leadership could be described using the Eastern taoist notion of yin and yang. Yin is the feminine, receptive, responsive subtle aspect of each person, whereas yang is the masculine, outgoing, creative, assertive aspect of leadership.

The transactional leader is yin; the transformational leader is yang. The total leader has the ability to be both transactional and transformational as is appropriate to the specific situation. Although most leaders have a personal tendency to be more inclined toward either a transactional or transformational style, both types are needed for quality leadership.

Transactional leadership is characterized here as the ability to understand the needs and abilities of specific individuals and to utilize group dynamics and teamwork to create a greater source of power from the total group than is possible by combining the sum of the individual members. Elsewhere, it is simply described as being strictly involved with a literal transaction; here, however, it is defined as being attuned to the relationship component.

Synergy is often used to describe such an increased team effect. Effective transactional leaders are adept at utilizing the subtle power of encouragement for improved human relations, with corresponding enhanced performance as a consequence.

> "The goal of a leader is not to exert force,
> but to empower his or her followers;
> leaders are more like holy men than muscle men."
>
> James MacGregor Burns

A LEADERSHIP BY ENCOURAGEMENT SOCIAL SKILLS APPROACH

Some of the encouraging leader's attributes that leaders need in order to be transactional developers of people are:

1. *Oral communication skills*, such as speaking, listening, and running staff meetings and company-wide meetings.

2. *Written communication skills*, for memos, reports, and letters.

3. *Accept imperfections in oneself and in others.* Criticize privately, praise publicly, and give credit to others generously while taking the blame for whatever goes wrong. One sign of a top-notch leader is the capacity to withstand pain and ambiguity.

4. *Prepare people* for upgrading and for new responsibilities.

5. *Report regularly to employees about benefits*, so that benefits will not be taken for granted.

6. *Teach* staff members to be socially sensitive and aware of the attitudes, problems, and successes of subordinates.

7. *Establish performance reviews that stress social as well as technical skills.*

8. *Maintain pay levels, promotions, and pay raises that reward leadership* as well as invention and technical productivity.

9. *Demonstrate the capacity to discipline and control as well as show empathy for and understand employees.*

THE ENCOURAGING LEADER: A SUMMARY OF DISTINGUISHING CHARACTERISTICS

The following is a list of the encouraging leader's distinguishing characteristics. The theory and practice of encouragement will be described more fully in subsequent chapters.

Encouraging leaders:

1. See situations as challenges and opportunities instead of problems

2. Can identify the positive potential in every situation

3. Respect individuality and identify similarities

4. Give recognition and understand the power of positive feedback

5. Respond and communicate congruently

   A. Say what they mean

   B. Mean what they say

6. Develop and encourage responsibility in others

7. Provide positive performance reviews

8. Participate as equals

9. Move from power over others to power with them and replace the traditional language of power (control, direct, punish, threaten, order, demand) with a new problem-solving vocabulary (conflict resolution, influencing, persuasion, collaboration, cooperation, joint decision making, obtaining agreement, winning employees over, agreeing to disagree)

KEY POINTS

1. It requires courage to risk forming one's own company.

2. Successful organizations attend to both the technical and the emotional needs of their employees.

3. As Naisbitt notes, the more "high tech" a company becomes, the more important "high touch" interpersonal relationships on the job become.

4. Herzberg distinguished "motivators" (intrinsic elements such as interesting work, responsibility, recognition, and advancement) from "hygiene" factors (extrinsic factors such as the physical work environment, salary, supervision, conflict and pressures, and job security).

5. McGregor's Theory X states that people are primarily motivated by money, benefits, or the threat of punishment; Theory Y assumes that people are basically self-directed and will be responsible and creative at work if properly motivated. Ouchi's Theory Z combines the best of Eastern and Western business practices.

LEADERSHIP BY ENCOURAGEMENT APPLICATIONS

1. Review the five leadership trends for the 1990s. Which ones have already affected your organization? With which specific items do you most strongly agree or disagree? Develop an action plan to identify specific attitudes and/or behaviors you can initiate to more fully actualize these trends in your organization.

2. Using the list of distinguishing characteristics of encouraging leaders as a guide, rank yourself on a scale of 1 to 10 (1 = low, 10 = high) for the nine characteristics listed. Contemplate one or two examples that typify each rating you gave yourself. Make a commitment to work on improving just one of your scores. Be as specific as possible in identifying the actual behaviors or attitudes necessary for the desired changes to occur. Then visualize a situation in which the change has already happened.

ENCOURAGEMENT SKILLS

1. Review the five trends presented in this chapter. What specific skills do you believe are necessary to successfully demonstrate each trend?

2. An important skill is the ability to generalize an area of competence to an area of challenge.

   A. Give yourself a current effectiveness rating from 1 to 10 (1 = low, 10 = high) on each of the five trends.

   B. Consider your *highest* rating. What specific skills were necessary to achieve it?

   C. Consider your *lowest* rating. Try to generalize a skill from Item B above to Item C. For example, a score of 9 in human capital might include the skill of being able to differentiate the abilities of team members. Contrast a human capital self-rating of 9 with a feminine leadership self-rating of 5. The ability to generalize the skill of differentiating individual abilities would include the ability to catch oneself making stereotypical male/female gender statements, as opposed to seeing men and women as individuals.

   D. List one specific skill you can generalize from your highest to your lowest ranking.

REFERENCES

1. Verespej, M., "When workers get new roles." *Industry Week*, 241(3), 1992, p. 11.

2. Eckerson, W., "Challenging environment keeps workers motivated." *Network World*, 8(2), 1991, pp. 25–26.

3. Jain P., Fanrowscast words." *Information Week*, August 1994.

4. Bhide, A., "How entrepreneurs craft strategies that work." *Harvard Business Review*, April 1994.

5. Meeks F. and Sullivan H., "If at first you don't succeed." *Forbes*, November 1992, p. 172.

6. Naisbitt, J. and Aburdene, P., *Megatrends 2000*, New York: Avon Books, 1990.

7. Naisbitt, J., *Megatrends*, New York: Warner, 1982.

8. Davis, Andi, "Entrepreneurs: breaking out of the mold." *Florida Business–Tampa Bay*, February 1990, p. 14.

9. Kao R., *Iacocca: An Autobiography*, New York: Bantam Books, 1984.

10. Cunningham, J., Barton, K., and Lischeron, J., "Defining entrepreneurship." *Journal of Small Business Management*, January 1991, p. 45.

11. Buskirk, R., *The Entrepreneur's Handbook*, Los Angeles: Robert Bryan, Inc., 1985.

12. Herzberg, F., *Work and the Nature of Man*, Cleveland, OH: World, 1966.

13. McGregor, D., *The Human Side of Enterprise*, New York: McGraw-Hill, 1960.

14. Ouchi, W., *Theory Z: How American Businesses Meet the Japanese Challenge*, Reading, MA: Addison-Wesley, 1981.

15. "Managing the healthy association." *Association Management*, August 1993.

16. Bennis, W. and Nanus, B., *Leaders: The Strategies for Taking Charge*, New York: Harper & Row, 1985.

17. Garfield, C., *Peak Performers: The Heroes of American Business*, New York: William Morrow, 1986.

18. Kogod, S., "Managing diversity in the workplace." *The 1992 Annual: Developing Human Resources*, San Diego, CA: Pfeiffer & Company, 1992, pp. 241–249.

19. Simons, G., Vazquez, C., and Harris, D., *Transcultural Leadership Empowering the Diverse Workplace*, Houston: Gulf Publishing, 1993.

20. "Investing in people." *The Economist,* March 26, 1994, p. 85.

21. Jacobs, N., *Success and Betrayal: The Crisis of Women in Corporate America,* New York: Touchstone/Simon and Schuster, 1987.

22. Nelton, S., "Men, women and leadership." *Nation's Business,* 79(5), 1991, pp. 16–22.

23. Rosener, J., "Ways women lead." *Harvard Business Review,* 68(6), 1991, pp. 119–125.

24. Haddock, C., "Transformational leadership and the employee discipline process." *Hospital and Health Services Administration,* June 1989.

25. Bass, B., "From transactional to transformational leadership." *Management for the 90's,* New York: American Management Association, 1991, pp. 101–113.

26. Ciampa, D., *Total Duality,* Reading, MA: Addison-Wesley, 1992, p. 218.

3

THE PSYCHOLOGY OF
PEOPLE AT WORK

"Employee motivation is a complex science,
but its foundations rest on the simple recognition that
we all need to feel important in some phase of our lives."

Terrence Deal and Allen Kennedy (1982)

INTRODUCTION

Leadership is a person-to-person skill, and each person has his or her own unique style relative to applying the skill. Many management challenges are people issues, and the ability to apply practical behavioral science theory to specific work-related situations characterizes the most successful leaders. Applied behavioral science can be invaluable in providing clues to understanding employee behavior and motivating workers toward enhanced self-esteem and increased productivity.

This chapter provides a theoretical overview to the entire book by summarizing what we have found significant in our roles as consulting psychologists to various organizations. Although we utilize many different psychological techniques, we have found one useful approach to business issues based on the work of the noted psychiatrists Alfred Adler and Rudolf Dreikurs.

SUPER LEADERSHIP

In *An Introduction to the Theory and Practice of Life-Style Assessment,* Eckstein uses the acronym SUPER to represent fundamental Adlerian principles.[1] The letters stand for the following:

Social interest

Unity

Private logic

Equality

Reasons

Social Interest
U
P
E
R

Social interest is characterized by a willingness to cooperate with others for the common good of all—the universal interrelatedness of all human beings. The term "humanistic identification" has also been described as a feeling of close kinship with other human beings in the present as well as a strong affinity for the human race as a whole, past, present, and future. High social interest in the workplace connotes a sense of belonging, cooperation, and responsibility.[2]

Adler said that work is one of the three basic tasks of living that are encountered by everyone. An organization is a social system, much like one's family. Much of an individual's own personal power, status, income, and title relate to this crucial life task. Most people spend one-third to one-half of their time at work. A person's work is a significant contributor to his or her self-concept, and a person's sense of competence and adequacy is related to the kind and level of work he or she does. When we meet someone new, we frequently ask, "What kind of work do you do?"

> "**Y**ou can have everything in life you want
> if you will just help enough people get what they want."
>
> Zig Ziglar

An individual's first and primary social group is the family. With this orientation, people tend to create family-type structures in the workplace.

As parent figures, top executives help to create the work environment by establishing and modeling their (or corporate) values, standards, and procedures. If top management demands perfection or engages in blaming or punishment for mistakes, then initiative, exploration, inventiveness, independence, and expressiveness will most likely be constricted. The freedom to try and to make mistakes is essential to courageous inventiveness and productivity.

In the space below, graphically represent your own family of origin in the form of a family tree. List your parents, grandparents, and any siblings. If you have influential cousins, aunts, uncles, etc., include them in your diagram.

Now graphically illustrate yourself in your own organizational workplace. Put yourself in your proper place in the hierarchy of your company.

After you have completed both illustrations, answer the following questions:

1. Are there any similarities or common themes between your family of origin and your current workplace?

_____

_____

_____

2. Are there any "mother," "father," or "sibling" figures in your current organization?

_____

_____

_____

To illustrate the process, consider the personal illustration of co-author Daniel Eckstein. In his family of origin, he was the oldest of four children. As the oldest, he was often "in charge" when his parents were away. His other three siblings formed one subgroup, while his parents were another. He was thus in the middle between the two subgroups. He was also a bit of a loner, not really fitting into either group.

In his current work, he is a consulting psychologist in private practice about 25 percent of the time (the "loner" syndrome again). When he teaches at various universities, he is again in the middle between the administrators (parents) and students (younger siblings). Thus, he finds many parallels between his family of origin and his current job. How about you? What are the similarities and differences between your family and your job?

> "There's no better way to keep someone doing things
> the right way than by letting him or her know
> how much you appreciate their performance."
>
> Sam Walton

Thomas Edison failed in 94 percent of the experiments he initiated. Abraham Lincoln was defeated in his first 28 attempts for public office before finally winning two races: senator from Illinois and President of the United States!

An enlightened top management can help to create an atmosphere of honesty, acceptance, humor, and openness by establishing a reward system that values certain types of work behaviors.

"**Y**ou are not here merely to make a living, you are here in order to enable the world to live more amply, with greater vision, with a finer spirit of hope and achievement. You are here to enrich the world, and you impoverish yourself if you forget the errand."

Woodrow Wilson

There are specific feelings and thoughts associated with social interest. Leadership *feelings* associated with high social interest include:

1. **Belonging**—Instilling a feeling of trust as part of an interdependent organizational family team

2. **Commonality**—Finding the similarities rather than the polarized differences with others

3. **Optimism**—Believing that the work in general and the specific workplace in particular can be better

Leadership thoughts associated with social interest include:

1. The Golden Rule (I treat other employees as I would like to be treated by them).

2. My personal, professional, or organizational aspirations can be attained in harmony with others instead of stepping on or over them to get there.

3. The prosperity and survival of our organization, our nation, indeed, our world depend on the willingness of everyone to work together.

4. The ultimate measure of my leadership will be the extent to which I promoted the welfare of my total organizational community.[3]

Riles Rules of the Reverse 20/80

"**W**hen a successful organization becomes infected with the disease of Me, people who create 20 percent of the results will begin believing they deserve 80 percent of the rewards."

Pat Riley

Social interest, self-confidence, and optimal mental health are interrelated in effective leaders. The more one behaves, feels, and thinks as

described above, the more other workers will positively respond. Enhanced self-confidence compounds social interest, all of which produces
a feeling of happiness and well-being on the job and at home. Many
organizations have contributed much to the betterment of humanity (for
example, the Lions Club with vision, the Rotary with polio, and the
Shriners with their children's hospitals).

> "**M**utual aid is as much a law of animal life as mutual struggle."
>
> Prince Krapotkin

Social interest in the workplace translates to a genuine caring and
concern for others. It is highly correlated with leadership by encouragement because when people feel appreciated, valued, and a part of a larger
organization, the optimal utilization of their talents is possible.

> "**W**e were not meant to stand alone. We need to belong—to
> something or someone. Only where there is a mutual commitment
> will you find people prepared to deny themselves for the good of
> others....Loneliness may be the real disease of the next century, as
> we live alone, work alone, and play alone, insulated by our mo-
> dem, our walkman, or our television. The Italians may be wise to
> use the same word for both alone and lonely, for the first ultimately
> implies the second. It is no longer clear where we connect or to
> what we belong. If, however, we belong to nothing, the point of
> striving is hard to see...."
>
> Charles Handy

Social Interest
Unity
P
E
R

"The whole is greater than the sum of its parts" is one way to describe
a person's total personality. Everyone has personal beliefs about life in
general, other people, and oneself. The effective leader realizes that each
worker is a unified or whole individual. The effective leader also knows
that one of the highest forms of personnel management is the skill of
empathy, or the ability to understand an employee's lifestyle and then
understand and predict the impact of that lifestyle at work.

Consider the challenge that the following two workers pose for their
supervisor. Harry's basic convictions could be summarized as "Life is full

of pain, suffering, tragedy, and eventual death. Other workers generally compete with me and cause me not to get promotions. I am afraid that I will be laid off because of reductions in the work force if the economy stays the way it's been." Conversely, Marvin's basic beliefs are "Life is full of fun, adventure, excitement, and new opportunities at work. Other employees teach me valuable, creative, problem-solving approaches. I'm confident that if I'm laid off here, I will find other meaningful employment suited to my skills and interests."

Despite wanting to establish fair work standards, an effective leader would show awareness of the basic beliefs of Harry and Marvin by personalizing a leadership style for each. Obviously, Harry is more discouraged and may need extra attention and support lest his fears affect his performance.

The Number One Priority

What is most important in my quest to belong? What must I most urgently avoid? These questions characterize what has been called the number one priority.[4]

The four priorities are *comfort, pleasing, control,* and *superiority.* None is better than the others. Each has its assets and its price to be paid. The resulting four different worker styles are as follows:

1. ***Comfort***—Employees motivated primarily by comfort want to avoid stress, responsibility, and expectations at all costs. They take few risks and rarely volunteer for new projects. Their assets are that they are typically easygoing, they make few demands, and they tend to mind their own business. Leaders are often bored or irritated with such workers if their productivity diminishes and they develop a pampered, "keep things safe and cozy for me" attitude. Effective, encouraging leaders can help such people to take small steps toward taking risks.

2. ***Pleasing***—Some employees want the leader to approve of them. Their assets include being friendly and considerate; they frequently volunteer and generally do what the leader expects of them. Leaders are often initially pleased with such friendly, compliant people. Later, exasperation results from the worker's demand for attention and approval and the tendency to interpret the boss's slightest frown as personal rejection. A pleasing employee is typically anxious because his or her personal happiness too often depends on the approval of co-workers or leaders. Although such a desire to

please may be personally gratifying to the leader, the cost is lack of an honest relationship; true opinions are too often withheld for fear of rejection. An encouraging leaders invites a pleasing worker to regain his or her own sense of self-regard without having to be personally recognized by the boss.

3. ***Control***—Some employees typically strive to control by exerting influence over themselves, others, and the work environment. Humiliation is to be avoided at all costs. Assets include being highly controlled, leadership potential, good organizational abilities, and productivity. Leaders often feel challenged and angered by such individuals. Specific limitations of overcontrol include diminished creativity, lack of spontaneity, and social distance between peers and supervisors. Encouraging leaders need to avoid power plays with such individuals whenever possible, encourage internal mastery and control, and give power and leadership responsibilities whenever possible.

4. ***Superiority***—Some people feel a need to be better, more competent, more often right, and more useful than others. Such individuals are knowledgeable, precise, and generally persevering. Meaninglessness is the major organizational issue to avoid. Workers displaying superiority often feel overburdened, overresponsible, and overinvolved. An encouraging leader can use a cognitive approach to confront the irrational belief that one must be best or one is worthless. Striving to improve oneself is a positive endeavor; too often, however, a self-serving person cannot share in the successes of others because it simply becomes another challenge to do better.

The ultimate goal of an effective leader is not to try to change an employee's number one priority. Rather, by having an awareness of his or her own style and those of his or her employees, a leader can better help each employee to perceive the responses that the employee's style evokes in others, the price one pays for such a style, the potential impact on the employee's working relationship with the leader, and the potential for diminished productivity.

In summary, unity of one's actions is reflected in a general style of approach to work. Unity implies that the employee is a whole person, for whom work is only one part of life. Too many jobs consume workers and leave little time for them to develop other aspects of their lives. Good leaders are sensitive to the impact that personal life crises can have on job performance. The effective leader also is sensitive enough to observe and respect various personality orientations and their effect on the job.

Social Interest
Unity
Private Logic
E
R

> "**W**e don't see things as they are, we see things as we are."
>
> Anais Nin

Closely related to the holistic, integrated notion of a personal style on the job is what Adler called "private logic," a personal filter consisting of one's values, preferences, wants, and needs. All actions are based on this filter. Thus, external events are filtered through each person's internal, subjective frame of reference. In such a way, everyone distorts or shapes situations to conform with internal attitudes.

> "**Y**ou cannot consistently perform in a manner
> which is inconsistent with the way you see yourself."
>
> Zig Ziglar

The following analogy illustrates the filters that form our private logic. Imagine that you are given the task of finding out the size of the fish in Lake Michigan. You go to the lake to gather a sample of the fish. Your net has a four-inch mesh. After you gather some fish, you write your findings in a report: "The fish in Lake Michigan are four inches in diameter or bigger." Let's say a friend of yours is given the same assignment, but his net has a two-inch mesh. His report reads, "The fish in Lake Michigan are two inches in diameter or bigger." Which report is right? Both? What are you and your friend reporting on—the size of the fish? No. Each of you is reporting on the size of the net you used. The size of the net you use determines the size of the fish you can collect.

We have nets in our heads. These nets are not made of threads, but rather of past learning, past experiences, motives, fears, desires, and interests. These nets act as a filter, and the stimuli from our environment go through that filter to be perceived. Of course, each one of us has our own little net, our own little personal, individual filter. Even though we may be placed in the same environment, we will not see it in the same way since we filter different aspects. Most of us are not even aware that this filtering process is happening. Many of us have defective filters, filters that are so clogged that we see very little of what's going on. Some of us have filters that distort the stimuli that come to us from the environment.

The important thing to remember, however, is that *whenever we make a comment about something, we are not describing the something, but rather our net, our filter.* When we say that a painting is beautiful, we are not commenting on the painting as much as ourselves, our tastes, and our value systems.[5]

The successful leader begins to understand and recognize the various "nets" in his or her own head as well as those of individual employees. A truly empathic person can go outside his or her own orientations to perceive, if not truly understand, the personal wants, needs, and values of others.

> "Each of us has many, many maps in our head, which can be divided into two main categories: maps of the way things are, or realities, and maps of the way things should be, or values. We interpret everything we experience through these mental maps."
>
> Stephen Covey

Organizations also have private logic that reflects their formal and informal norms, values, needs, and ethics. Such basic beliefs have a profound impact on customer satisfaction. Cynthia Potter, a consultant and former vice president of training for Northwest Airlines, has devised the following equation to summarize the relationship of the basic beliefs of the organizational culture and customer satisfaction:[6]

Elements of the Approach

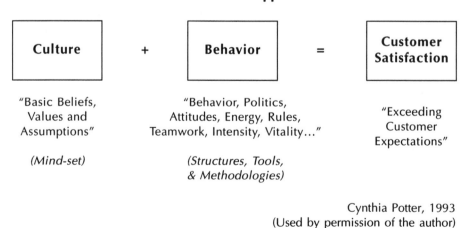

Culture	+	Behavior	=	Customer Satisfaction
"Basic Beliefs, Values and Assumptions"		"Behavior, Politics, Attitudes, Energy, Rules, Teamwork, Intensity, Vitality..."		"Exceeding Customer Expectations"
(Mind-set)		*(Structures, Tools, & Methodologies)*		

Cynthia Potter, 1993
(Used by permission of the author)

Consider the following contrasting organizational beliefs. The first reflects a discouraging Theory X approach.

Basic Beliefs	+	Behavior	=	What the Customer Sees:
"I'm not authorized..."		CYA		Needs not met on spot
"That's not my job..."		Many levels of approval		Can't get answers to questions
"People are always complaining..."		Defensive behavior Ignoring customers Little patience		Rude employees Lack of attention
"Quality costs too much."		Budget cuts Cutting corners Lack of training No resources		Technical breakdowns Shabby appearance Uninformed employees
"If we make our numbers, we're doing great..."		Manage using financial data Down-sizing to control costs Short-term budget cuts		Impatient employees Longer waits "on-hold"

Cynthia Potter, 1993
(Used by permission of the author)

An approach to customers based on a Theory Y, encouraging attitude is summarized by Potter as follows:

Basic Beliefs	+	Behavior	=	What the Customer Sees:
"The customer is always right" "Exceed customer expectations."		Customer-focused perception Treat customers as "guests" Know what the customer wants Clear communications		Satisfied/ Delighted/ Amazed Customers
"Quality is my job..." "I make a difference."		Personal responsibility Ownership Teamwork Continual improvement Personal development		Motivated/ Energized/Satisfied/ Involved/ Committed Employees
"Process focused..."		Prevention oriented Proactive vs. reactive Long-term thinking Decisions based on facts		Cost competitive/ Efficient/Consistent/ Smooth-running Operation

Cynthia Potter, 1993
(Used by permission of the author)

> "**R**ather than defining strategies in terms of your competition,
> then you define them in terms of customers
> and how you deliver value to them."
>
> K. Ohmae

Most managers focus on the collective groups of customers that comprise a market, thereby adapting a relatively impersonal attitude toward the marketplace. Like many other aspects of business, the manager thinks about markets in fairly analytical and quantitative terms and is comfortable with such terms as market share, market segment, market growth, market life cycle, etc.

> "**T**he leader, in contrast, prefers a more quantitative and human view of the marketplace and likes to think of a market in terms of individual customers. The leader's soul takes into account the human side of customers—the feelings, emotions, needs and wants that cause customers to purchase a product or service."
>
> C. Hackman
> *Mind of a Manager, Soul of a Leader*

Thus, employee, leader, and organizational belief systems are the components of an encouraging or discouraging organizational private logic.

Social Interest
Unity
Private Logic
Equality
R

Equal political, economic, and social rights are the essence of democratic ideology. Equality is also a pivotal principle of the encouraging leader psychology, as the authoritarian stance is increasingly replaced by a dialogue between equals in an atmosphere of mutual respect, candor, and acceptance.

Adler's term "masculine protest" was formulated as a precursor to the sexism that the women's movement was founded to fight. In a culture that inherently values what is "masculine" over what is "feminine," both men and women suffer negative consequences. Equality may be explained as a horizontal rather than vertical way of approaching people.[7]

The horizontal approach views all people as equally worthy of respect and consideration, although people are obviously unequal in other ways. Such equality does not mean sameness, but means that each human being's birthright is unconditional respect and dignity.

In contrast, the vertical approach measures people from a "one up" or "one down" perspective. "Better than/less than" characterizes the vertical plane, while "different from" is the horizontal perspective. An orange is different from (horizontal), not better than (vertical), an apple.

Inferiority and superiority are simply two sides of the same coin for Adler. Both result in a feeling of separateness or disconnection from others. The horizontal view leads to contentment and happiness, while the vertical view means one is "on a ladder," viewing others as "up" or "down." Social interest is related to mental health based on equality and democratic interactions, in contrast to striving for personal superiority above others.

Equality in the workplace does not imply sameness. Effective leadership is not diminished by a philosophy that respects all human beings as worthwhile. The growing number of sexual harassment suits, unequal pay for women, racial discrimination, and cultural/national discrimination are evidence that mutual dignity and respect still need to be core organizational values. Equality is a crucial organizational norm. It has nothing to do with rank, status, education, or salary. It has everything to do with employee satisfaction, which affects customer satisfaction.

Personal superiority issues also have a multicultural correlate. Sociologists use the term *ethnocentrism* to refer to the personal preferences of one's own particular group or cultural norm. For example, an American who was in Japan attended a funeral. When he observed food being placed on the casket, he said to his host, "Why do you put food on the casket? The person surely can't eat it." His Japanese host replied, "Why do you Americans put flowers on your caskets? The person surely can't smell them." An acupuncturist from India was told, "You are a good doctor even if you are from the East."

Ethnocentrism relates to regional, cultural, and national feelings of superiority or inferiority and is a major cause of strife between various cultures. In contrast, effective leaders have a sense of equality with others based on mutual dignity and basic respect.

Social Interest
Unity
Private Logic
Equality
Reasons

A search for reasons for, or motivators of, personal behavior includes the belief that all behavior is purposeful or goal-directed and that we all strive for significance or perfection.

The most apparently self-defeating actions have some type of payoff. For example, one possible reward for never completing a project is that it can never be judged. Another benefit is that the worker attracts attention from his or her supervisor and perhaps gets help in completing the assignment. A third payoff is that it could verify the worker's low self-esteem.

Realizing that every action fulfills some function can help in understanding employee goals and intentions. Aligning employee goals such as security, promotion, recognition, control, and attention with organizational goals is a challenge for leaders. However, the resultant congruence of goals produces energy and interest.

In practicing such a principle, the leader asks, "For what purpose is he or she doing that?" or "What is the possible payoff to him or her for engaging in that behavior?" Just as a small child with deaf parents throws a temper tantrum with all the typical facial expressions and bodily gestures without making a sound, so too do workers use what is functional. People do not lose their tempers; they consciously or unconsciously "throw them away" for such purposes as putting others into their service, punishing others, demanding attention, or displaying frustration or inadequacy. By seeking to discover the payoff or purpose of a dysfunctional behavior, a leader can more readily understand and deal with it.

"Harry just can't seem to tolerate success," was the observation of a manager after a quarterly performance appraisal. Indeed, it seemed that catastrophe struck Harry each time he received acknowledgment or a possible promotion. Once, he mysteriously lost a crucial report; another time, he accidentally noted a meeting in his appointment book at ten o'clock instead of nine o'clock.

What possible payoff could all these misfortunes have for Harry? One possibility is that he will never actually be promoted. His self-defeating filter tells him that he does not deserve a promotion or that he cannot handle the added responsibilities, so the purpose of his misfortunes is to prevent him from being promoted.

Harry internally doubted his ability to handle a promotion. Since there was dissonance or inconsistency between his attitude and his behavior, he was relieved when he did something wrong, which proved that he had been right all along. Thus, the payoffs for making a mistake were confirmation of his belief and the safety of his old job.

An effective leader is able to see the big picture, one that extends beyond the specific disruptive behaviors of employees to the underlying motivators or payoffs for even the most seemingly self-defeating behaviors. The encouraging leader uses a specific set of behaviors that can help combat such discouragement.

KEY POINTS

1. Social interest (or humanistic identification) is the ability to consider the needs of others, a feeling of connectedness to people.

2. Employees, leaders, and organizations have unified themes or lifestyles that reflect personal values, wants, motivators, and needs.

3. Comfort, pleasing, control, and superiority have been identified as number one priorities of lifestyle.

4. An understanding of an individual's private logic, or personal filter, is a key leadership attribute. It is synonymous with empathy, or the ability to perceive the subjective world of someone else.

5. Equality, a feeling of mutual respect and dignity, is a fundamental characteristic of effective, encouraging leaders and effective, encouraging organizations.

6. Values of leaders and organizations that encourage are characterized by a horizontal perspective based on mutual respect. Conversely, discouraging leaders and organizations are characterized by a vertical perspective based on superiority and inferiority.

THE ENCOURAGING LEADER APPLICATIONS

1. Write in your journal examples of social interest you have observed in your organization. How do you personally demonstrate social interest? What steps can you take to improve your own humanistic identification toward other individuals in your organization?

2. Reflect on your personal filter, your own private logic. What are some of your own key values, motivators, and needs? What are some of your own idiosyncrasies?

3. Compare and contrast your most challenging and your most successful employees. How are they different? How do those differences reflect conflicts with your own values? Now identify the similarities between you, your "star," and your "challenge." How do your filters contribute to your perceptions of these individuals? Try to develop an approach to encouraging the "challenging" employee by learning more about his or her personal style.

4. Refer to the list of number one priorities Which one is most characteristic of you? Describe how you behaviorally exhibit that priority on the job. Do the same for each of your employees.

5. What are your prevailing organizational values? Compare them to the horizontal and vertical chart. What are some strategies for moving from the vertical to the horizontal plane from an organizational perspective?

ENCOURAGEMENT SKILLS

1. Social interest or humanistic identification is an attitude and a skill. Identify your most challenging worker. In what specific ways could you demonstrate more social interest in that person?

   For one week, develop an action plan to demonstrate your increased social interest.

   Seven-day follow-up observations include:

2. Paradox is an important leadership skill. It is the ability to find a connecting truth in two apparently contradictory statements. For example, consider the concept of equality. Try to identify the paradox that despite unique and separate personalities, there are certain unifying themes characteristic of all people in your organization. Demonstrate the skill of paradox by contrasting key differences with similarities.

   a. Core differences:

   b. Core similarities:

REFERENCES

1. Eckstein, D. and Baroth, L., *An Introduction to the Theory and Practice of Life-Style Assessment,* Dubuque, IA: Kendall-Hunt, 1996.

2. O'Connell, W., "Humanistic identification." *Individual Psychology,* 47(1), 1991, pp. 26–27.

3. Kaplan, H., "A guide for explaining social interest to laypersons." *Individual Psychology,* 47(1), 1991, pp. 82–85.

4. Dewey, E., *Basic Applications of Adlerian Psychology,* Coral Springs, FL: CMTI Press, 1978.

5. Myers, G. and Myers, M., *The Dynamics of Human Communication,* New York: McGraw-Hill, 1973.

6. Potter, C., *Adlerian Practices in Organizations Today,* unpublished manuscript, 1993.

7. Sicher, L., "Education for freedom." *American Journal of Individual Psychology,* 11, 1955, pp. 97–103.

4

IMPROVING LEADERSHIP AND MANAGERIAL PERFORMANCE

"**B**e willing to make decisions.
That's the most important quality in a good leader.
Don't fall victim to what I call the
'ready–aim–aim–aim–aim' syndrome."

T. Boone Pickens

INTRODUCTION

This chapter presents a model for leadership/management interventions. The model depicts a systematic approach to leadership. It is circular, based on the premise that successful completion takes one from start to finish and then leads back to start for a new beginning at a deeper level (see Appendix #7, Processing Solutions: The Improving Management Performance Cycle).

The improving management performance cycle integrates the encouragement philosophy. The phases of the improving management performance model are as follows:

1. Identify the issue

2. Inventory assets

3. Set and align goals

4. Appraise performance

5. Consequences

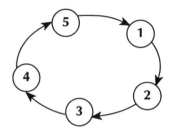

THE IMPROVING MANAGEMENT PERFORMANCE CYCLE

Improving management performance is a process to help managers think systematically about real issues and problems. It shows them how they can amass their resources and assets and establish goals that can be aligned with their employees' goals.

The process includes a method for appraising performance and implementing consequences based on the result of the appraisal. These consequences are logical consequences: encouragement, praise, and reprimands.

THE IMPROVING MANAGEMENT PERFORMANCE PROCESS

Phase 1: Identify the Issue

Whenever a problem is presented to a leader, the first step is to clearly identify the issue. The leader then seeks access to as much information about the issue as possible, looking for facts that are not immediately apparent.

It is important to establish operational goals with each employee in order to establish sound criteria for appraisal and managerial decision making. With clear operational goals, employees can help the leader to identify how things are progressing compared to the established standard of performance. When operational goals are not being met, the leader needs to take steps to correct the performance.

In identifying the real issue in any problem situation, a manager must decide whether the problem is one of *skills,* one of *motivation,* or a combination of the two. A skill deficit will not be changed by a motivational or attitudinal approach. The employee must be brought up to the necessary skill level if the operational goal is to be met.

In other instances, the problem may be primarily motivational. Employees may be in conflict with goals because they want to control people or the situation. They may be more concerned with comfort than with meeting the established criteria, or their desire to please others may interfere with performance. Whenever a performance deficit is based on motivation, the leader needs to discover the motive or goal that is keeping the employee from being more productive. Once this has been identified, the leader can talk constructively and productively with the employee about particular priorities.

For example, if an employee has a problem with control and is in conflict with his or her immediate supervisor, productivity may be affected. The productivity of a work group also may be reduced if someone slows production down because of excessive or unrealistic standards.

If a problem is caused by an individual's personal motivations, the Kern Lifestyle Scale can be helpful. It can be administered and scored in minutes. The Lifestyle Scale identifies such characteristics as control, perfectionism, the need to please, and the need to be a victim or a martyr.[1] Further insight into dysfunctional personal motivation is provided by Earnie Larsen and Jeanette Goodstein in *Who's Driving Your Bus: Codependent Business Behaviors of Workaholics, Perfectionists, Martyrs, Tap Dancers, Caretakers, and People Pleasers.*[2]

Skill or Motivation? Using Situational Leadership as a Tool

Situational leadership is particularly useful in the initial step of identifying the issue. Hersey and Blanchard identify the two levels of a worker's ability to perform a task (task-relevant readiness) as skill (functional ability) and willingness (confidence and/or motivation). Readiness levels are defined as R_1 (low), R_2 (low to moderate), R_3 (moderate to high), and R_4 (high).

Hersey and Blanchard describe the appropriate leadership style as resulting from an assessment of the worker's task-relevant readiness. They identify four leadership styles: *telling* (S_1), *selling* (S_2), *participating* (S_3), and *delegating* (S_4). These are specific combinations of task-focused and relationship-focused leader behavior.[*]

Task-focused behavior involves defining the specific aspects of each task and explaining what, when, where, and how each task is to be

---

[*] For more information on this theory, contact The Center for Leadership Studies, 140 South Hickory Street, Escondido, CA 92024.

accomplished. Goal setting, organizing, setting time lines, directing, and controlling are specific examples of leader task behaviors.

Relationship behavior is meant to encourage, provide support, facilitate, reinforce, and reward. Communicating, facilitating interventions, actively listening, and providing feedback are relationship-oriented leader behaviors.

The "telling" leadership style is used with workers who are both unable and unwilling to take responsibility for the task. With such workers, the leader must provide specific, task-related instructions: who, what, how, when, and where. This is high-task/low-relationship leadership.

"Selling" is used with a worker who is willing but unable to do the task. This may be a motivational rather than a skill problem. The leadership style is characterized by high task instructions with increased relationship aspects in order to build motivation and buy-in and to encourage progress and reward accomplishment.

The "participating" leadership style is used when an employee is able but unwilling or insecure. This calls for low task behavior (the employee already knows what, how, etc.) and high relationship behavior, in order to encourage the employee's confidence and acceptance of responsibility for the task. Two-way communication and active listening occur in a supportive, nondirective environment. This style is called participating because the leader and follower share in decision making, with the main role of the leader as facilitator and communicator.

"Delegating" is the style to use with employees who are able, willing, and confident to take responsibility. At this high worker readiness level, little direction (task) or support (relationship) is needed from the manager. In fact, too much relationship behavior here may be seen as patronizing or interfering. The employee's sense of accomplishment and self-direction are his or her primary motivators.[3]

One of the most common and inappropriate leadership styles is a leader who starts out very structured and directive and then, in effect, "walks away" from managing the employee (behavior used inappropriately). When the abandoned worker makes mistakes or takes advantage of the overly permissive style, the leader then overreacts, reverting to overcontrol and overstructure. Workers in such an environment often are extremely uncertain of the rules and feel confused by the inconsistency.

A crucial first step in identifying the issue, then, is to assess the worker's readiness level by finding out if the situation is the result of an ability (skill) deficit, a motivational or confidence deficit, or a combination.

Technoculture and Skills Training

Laura Field has written a very practical book entitled *Skills Training for Tomorrow's Workforce*. She introduces the term "technoculture" in referring to the complex pattern of relations between technology and the social system in an organization. She uses the analogy of an iceberg to describe the skills that an employee uses to perform a particular job or learn a new competency area. Task skills are at the core of the iceberg and are mainly above the surface. Supporting this core, and mainly under the surface, are four other types of skills:

1. ***Task management skills***—Include activities such as planning an activity to minimize waste, performing a number of tasks in the appropriate order, or anticipating and avoiding problems

2. ***Work environment skills***—Such as working effectively within constraints or changing unhealthy, unsafe aspects of work

3. ***Workplace learning skills***—Such as being self-directed in learning, being adaptable to change, or encouraging workplace learning

4. ***Interpersonal skills***—Such as maintaining good work relations, working in a team, or discussing workplace issues and problems[5]

Four specific approaches to skills training are generally used in most organizations. Off-site training utilizes private training and schools, vocational training centers, local community colleges, universities, equipment manufacturers, and other agencies. Formal in-house training refers to structured programs that take place away from the actual job. On-the-job training occurs at the workplace under the guidance of an experienced employee, supervisor, or trainer.[4]

Field believes that traditional approaches to skills training often overemphasize task skills and treat under-the-surface skills indirectly or even ignore them altogether. The encouraging leader specifically addresses such "hidden" but crucial human skills.

A Case Study

Consider the following examples of the *same* dysfunctional employee behavior but for *different* reasons.

Mark and Lane are front-line supervisors in a data-processing company. Weekly reports summarizing production levels and inventory control are essential to the vice president. In the past month, both Mark and Lane have been late in submitting their reports.

In talking with Mark, the vice president determined that Mark was feeling insecure and inadequate. He was reluctant to submit his data because he was new on the job, despite his reputation as one of the most thorough and conscientious supervisors in his unit. In his new position, he was less sure of his data or how to submit the summaries. The vice president also noted perfectionist tendencies which caused Mark to withhold his information until he was absolutely certain of his statistics.

In contrast, a conversation with Lane revealed his thorough knowledge of the job, the data, and the actual report-writing process. The real issue was his unwillingness to complete the task. He disagreed about the actual need for the report and resented the memo that dictated how to write it. He also felt that there wasn't enough time to complete the task and that he had more pressing responsibilities.

In his conversation with the vice president, Lane expressed his resentment about how the demand was made. He also gave specific suggestions about how the summary could be improved. His failure to complete the project was his way of protesting the manner in which the assignment was made.

The same behavior, failure to complete the weekly report, was motivated by different things. Mark felt unskilled and a lack of confidence, whereas Lane was able but unwilling.

It is important to remember that the only way a leader can find the right solution is by identifying the real issue. All too often, leaders do not distinguish between skill and motivational problems. They may also lack an understanding of the purposive nature of human behavior. Without some recognition of an individual's priorities in terms of control, superiority, comfort, and pleasing and their resulting effect on morale and productivity, the leader may not discover the real issue. When the real issue has been identified, the leader can plan a suitable course of action.

Try to formulate intervention strategies based on the diagnoses that Mark is unable and insecure and Lane is able but unwilling to complete the request.

The following checklist* is useful in helping determine the skills versus motivation issues of the situational leadership model.[6]

---

* Roseman, E., "Situational leadership, flexibility is the key." *Medical Laboratory Observer,* January 1983, p. 62. Used by permission of the publisher.

A. Task
   ☐ Routine   ☐ Special

   1. How quickly must it be done?
      ☐ Very quickly
      ☐ Somewhat quickly
      ☐ No particular deadline

   2. How complex is it?
      ☐ The task is not complex, and the group knows how to do it
      ☐ The task is complex, and the group knows how to do it
      ☐ The task is somewhat complex, and the work group is uncertain how to do it

   3. Do you and your staff agree on the standards for the task?
      ☐ There is complete understanding and agreement
      ☐ There is fair understanding and agreement
      ☐ There is some disagreement or confusion
      ☐ There is much disagreement or confusion

B. Leader–member relations
   1. How friendly are relations between you and your staff?
      ☐ Friendly
      ☐ Somewhat friendly
      ☐ Somewhat unfriendly

   2. How cooperative has your staff been in the past?
      ☐ Very
      ☐ Fairly
      ☐ Somewhat
      ☐ Not very

   3. How compatible are your work attitudes with those of your staff?
      ☐ Very similar
      ☐ Fairly similar
      ☐ Somewhat different
      ☐ Very different

C. Staff issues
   1. How knowledgeable is your staff?
      ☐ Very
      ☐ Moderately
      ☐ Not very

2. How experienced is your staff?
   □ Very
   □ Moderately
   □ Not very

3. What is the level of responsibility of your staff?
   □ Strong sense of responsibility
   □ Somewhat low sense of responsibility
   □ Low sense of responsibility

4. How motivated is your staff?
   □ Strongly
   □ Somewhat
   □ Poorly

D. Power
   1. How great is your supervisory authority?
      □ Strong
      □ Adequate
      □ Low

   2. How dependent are your employees on your supervisory expertise?
      □ Very
      □ Somewhat
      □ Not at all

Phase 2: Inventory Assets

Phase 2 involves developing the capacity to identify some positive potential—any effort, interest, or latent talent. This is accomplished by developing the ability to formulate perceptual alternatives. A perceptual alternative
suggests the capacity to see the positive side in any situation. It is the
ability to see the glass as half full rather than half empty.

In any game in which one person wins and feels triumphant, another
will feel discouraged and defeated. The event is the same, but the
interpretation of the experience differs. Perceptual alternatives provide the
opportunity to ask what positive potential or possibility is available in a
particular situation. A perceived minus is often merely a plus waiting to
be redefined or reframed. Stubbornness can be seen as determination, or
resistance can be seen as commitment to a cause or position. The challenge is to turn a negative trait into a potential asset.

The following example demonstrates how an innovative teacher successfully helped to reframe a perceived negative attribute. It was written

at midnight on Thanksgiving evening as the author reflected on a formative event that occurred 35 years earlier.

A Tribute to Many Uncrowned Kings and Queens*

It was the spring of 1962. I was in the seventh grade at Johnnycake
Junior High School in Baltimore, section 7B to be precise. In earlier
years, classes had been called the "redbirds" and the "bluebirds" in
a vain attempt to avoid labeling one the smart class and the other
(mine) the dummy group. But we all knew who was who relative
to the hierarchy of redbirds and bluebirds. So in seventh grade the
pretense was dropped in favor of 7A and 7B.

All my neighborhood friends were in the coveted 7A class. As
for me, I was majoring in playground. I was also an "honor"
student, as in "yes, your honor, no your honor, I won't do that
anymore your honor..."

I was a classic left-handed, dyslexic, hyperactive boy who consistently received unsatisfactory scores in the category vaguely defined as self-control. D's masqueraded as B's; P's as Q's and M's
and N's were indistinguishable to me. Classes were much too long,
the desks far too small, and the outdoor activities way too short.
Like a prisoner about to be granted a three-month furlough prior to
returning to the cell I called a classroom desk, I was counting down
the days until June....

The teacher for both 7A and 7B was like a great redwood tree
to me, a colossal giant who at 6 feet 2 inches tall seemed twice as
awesome from my diminished vantage point. Mr. King was the
well-named title of our teacher. He was kind, knowledgeable, and
much revered by both sections 7A and 7B, a rare feat in and of itself
for any teacher.

One day, quite unexpectedly, Mr. King approached my friends
in 7A and said, "There is someone in 7B who is just as smart as any
of you. Trouble is, he's the kid who outruns all of you and knocks
the ball over the right-field fence."

Word of Mr. King's declaration reached me that afternoon as I
boarded the school bus. I remember a dazed, numb, shocked
feeling of disbelief. "Yeah, sure—you've got to be kidding," I
nonchalantly replied to my friends, but on a deeper, more subtle
level I remember the warm glow that came from the tiny flicker of
hope that had been ignited within my soul.

---

* From Eckstein, Daniel, *The Encouragement Process in Life-Span Development,* Dubuque,
IA: Kendall-Hunt, 1995.

Two weeks later, it was time for the dreaded book reports in front of the class. It was bad enough to turn in papers that only Mr. King read and graded. Alas, there was no place to hide when it came to oral book reports.

When my turn came, I solemnly stood before my classmates. I began slowly and awkwardly to speak about James Fenimore Cooper's epic book *The Pathfinder*. As I spoke, images of canoes on the western frontier of 18th century America collided with lush descriptions of the forest and the Native Americans who glided noiselessly over lakes and streams. No Fourth of July fireworks has ever surpassed the explosion that took place inside my head that day. It was electrifying!

Excitedly, I began trying to share my experience with my classmates. But just as I began a sentence about the canoes, another scene of the land collided with the Native Americans. I was only mid-way through one sentence before I jumped to another.

I was becoming "hyper" in my joy, and my incomplete sentences made no sense at all. The laughter of my classmates quickly shattered my inner fireworks. I was embarrassed and humiliated, and I wanted to either beat up my tormentors or run home and cry in my mother's arms. But long ago I had learned how to mask those feelings, so trying my best to become invisible and disappear, I started to return to my desk.

The laughter ceased at the sound of Mr. King's deep, compassionate voice. "You know, Danny" he reigned forth, "you have a unique gift, that being the ability to speak outwardly and to think inwardly at the same time. But sometimes your mind is filled with so much joy that your words just can't keep up with it. Your excitement is contagious. It's a wonderful gift that I hope you can put to good use some day."

There was a pause that seemed to linger forever as I stood stunned by Mr. King's words once more. And then it began— clapping and congratulatory cheers from my classmates as a miracle of transformation occurred within me.

Thirty years later, I take my turn to say thank you to all the nameless Mr. and Ms. Kings who are the teachers of our young people. I now have fancy sounding names like encouragement or turning a perceived minus into a plus to describe how Mr. King helped me reframe my life forever.

It has been said that the greatest use of a life is to spend it in a cause that will ultimately outlive it. Though often underpaid and faced with far too many students and far too few resources, I salute you, our teachers, and hope you and your community will take a moment to acknowledge that in many subtle ways you do make a difference!

Reframing a perceived negative into a positive is one way to focus on assets. Seeing different perspectives from different points of view is also important. Leaders need to understand that how a chairman of the board or a CEO perceives a problem differs from the way employees in advertising, marketing, or production do. By becoming aware of the problem-solving potential in the organization and by being in touch with the many varied assets and perceptions, a leader can help employees become positive forces for problem resolution.

While identifying each worker's assets and resources, leaders should consider how those various resources can either encourage or discourage the individual. For example, intelligence can be a plus in solving problems, but always being expected to be intelligent can be a burden.

A leader should help employees to find solutions to problems. A good place to start is by helping them develop self-assessments of their assets, resources, and potential. Then the leader should assist the employees in deciding exactly how each source of power can be applied.

Many people tend to be cautious or modest in identifying their own strengths. Suppose an employee performs satisfactorily at work 95 percent of the time and does not perform only 5 percent of the time. Because the employee is not competent 100 percent of the time, task competence may not be acknowledged as a strength. Focusing on deficiencies and limitations which are exceptions to the rule can reduce motivation, involvement, and commitment.

A second barrier to acknowledging an asset stems from the emphasis that some people place on being the best. In acknowledging their own skills, people often qualify their success by thinking that they must be the best in order to be truly valuable.

One technique to assist in affirming assets is to have the worker identify examples of previous successes or competence and then generalize the skill to present and future situations. If an individual was successful in one job, the leader can help to identify the specific skill involved and explore how this skill can be used in the current task.

Let's return to the example of Mark and Lane and their overdue reports. After identifying the specific issue with Mark as being a feeling of inadequacy, the vice president utilized the perceptual alternative to reframe Mark's discouragement. Specifically, the negative label (perfectionist) was reframed to a more encouraging one (desire to achieve by doing the job right). No behavior changed, but Mark's opinion of himself changed drastically.

Because the specific issue with Lane was motivational, the vice president acknowledged Lane's courage to stand up for his beliefs. The vice president engaged in active listening and took notes on Lane's suggestions. They developed an agreement regarding the supervision process.

Phase 3: Goal Setting and Goal Aligning

This leadership procedure is likely well within the skill range of every leader. First, clear performance standards that are achievable and that will secure the involvement of the employee need to be established. This suggests that performance standards and goals must be accepted, even desired, by employees if they are to result in enthusiastic, energetic involvement in achieving goals.

In any meeting with employees, the manager must have clear criteria for successful goal achievement. An opportunity to discuss and agree on goals should follow.

Autocratic leaders function as if they can set goals for their employees and the employees will accomplish them. Encouraging leaders recognize the need for employee cooperation, involvement, and enthusiasm from the start. Spending time with employees to agree on goals and establish specific, realistic standards is essential for long-range productivity.

At the end of any meeting devoted to discussion of the goals for the organization, the leader should write a brief statement of the purpose or goal of the ensuing work project and the specific goals of those employed at various levels. As work proceeds, these goals enable the employees to assess themselves in order to determine whether their behavior facilitates the stated goals.

Setting goals is essential to helping individuals know the specific desired behavior or performance. Goal setting is actually the flip-side or reverse of problem identification. Identifying a specific skill and/or motivational deficiency is the first step toward setting specific goals. It can be summarized as, "I am lacking... (deficiency), but I want... (goal setting) in order to... (desired outcome)."

James Champy suggests the following ten corporate/individual values:

1. Perform up to the highest measure of competence, always.

2. Take initiatives and risks.

3. Adapt to change.

4. Make decisions.

5. Work cooperatively as a team.

6. Be open, especially with information, knowledge, and news of forthcoming or actual "problems."

7. Trust, and be trustworthy.

8. Respect others (customers, suppliers, and colleagues) and one-self.

9. Answer for our actions, to accept responsibility.

10. Judge and be judged, reward and be rewarded, on the basis of performance.[7]

Using the Organizational Mission to Guide Goal Setting

Although it may seem simplistic, employees often disagree with or are confused about the primary focus and task of the organization. An organizational mission statement is a unifying force, or overarching goal, which all can use to formulate their own departmental and personal goals. An organizational mission statement is a clear, concise statement of what business the organization is in and the actual purpose or function the organization is attempting to fulfill. An organization should answer three primary questions when formulating a mission statement:

1. *What* function does the organization perform?

2. *For whom* does the organization perform the function?

3. *How* does the organization go about filling this function?

Many companies tend to answer the "what" question in terms of the goals or services produced (for example, bath soap), but the broader consideration is to describe the "what" in terms of customer needs the organization is attempting to meet. Instead of soap, the actual function becomes providing personal hygiene products to consumers, with possible future expansion into hair care products, after-bath moisturizers, etc.

The "who" involves clearly identifying the portion of the total potential customer base the organization sees as its primary target. The process of classifying the potential customer or client base and identifying the targeted portion is called market segmentation.

> "The consumer is our boss, quality is our work, and value for the money is our goal."
>
> The Quality Principle of Mars, Inc.

The "how" can involve a marketing strategy, a distribution system, customer services, or personalized selling. The "what," "who," and "how" must be included in any statement of organizational goals that is realistic, objective, and attainable. The answers provide leaders with a set of core priorities and guidelines.[8]

With these specific objectives as a guide, managers and organizational leaders can more clearly define their own goals and those of their employees. Goal alignment is the process of making the goals of management and workers consistent. One question for employees to consider is how is it in their self-interest to have common goals. Unilateral, top-down decisions may be necessary at times, but employees feel more involved and more responsible for outcomes when they are able to play a part in setting their own and their work unit's goals. With clear organizational goals, it is easier for leaders to work with employees in formulating mutual goals all down the line (see Appendix #7, Processing Solutions: The Improving Management Performance Cycle).

> "It seemed so much simpler in the days of the old corporate 'machine.' You hired people to work for you, so you chose them, judged them, and rewarded them for their ability to perform a specific task.
>
> That doesn't work anymore. Reengineering demands that we hire people to work with us, as part of a community of shared aspirations, ideals, and trust. The ability to perform a specific task isn't enough: today we need people who add value to every process they touch, and who bring values to our company."
>
> James Champy

Bob O'Neal, senior manager for the AT&T Universal Card University, describes three learning areas which further assist the alignment of corporate and employee values and goals.

> "The first one is people's ability to do their job. The second thing we try to do is communicate and reinforce our company's values, vision, and mission so that people will know what we believe in. Not only how to do the work, but in what philosophical framework we expect it to be done: how we expect that we will interact with each other and what our relationships with each other are.
>
> That's the cultural piece of our training, and it begins at the beginning. The whole recruitment process teaches people who we are as a company, and how we interact. Immediately we treat the people we are hiring as customers. We treat them as we would like to be treated, but also as we want them to treat customers."[9]

Phase 4: Appraise Performance

Once goals have been established and projects begun, leaders need a systematic and effective way to observe, evaluate, and give feedback on performance and progress. Too many leaders only occasionally observe what is happening with a project and have only an offhand impression of the status. A leader must be in a position to take systematic samples of what is happening, develop clear evaluations, and give appropriate feedback to employees.

Systematic performance appraisals are essential to business excellence. It is beneficial for leaders to develop feedback that is thorough, behaviorally specific, and clearly points to required action. Employees may have little or no knowledge of exactly what they are expected to accomplish at work. Performance appraisal should always be dictated by organizational goals. Both positive and negative feedback should describe actual behavior instead of generalized traits or perceived attitudes. Rewards for specific behaviors are more meaningful and motivating. If remedial action is required, it is necessary to describe exactly what behaviors or task functions are lacking and to be specific about what should be done to make them acceptable. Telling employees that they need to work harder or need to change their attitude does not tell them how to improve their performance.

> "Sink-or-swim is no more a sound policy in management than it is in the swimming pool. Water-wings are no good, either, just another form of command-and-control. The best policy is clear, measurable guidelines—swimming lessons, if you will."
>
> James Champy

Positive Performance Reviews

An encouraging leader uses performance reviews as an opportunity to provide mutual feedback. The evaluation considers the development of traits valued by the organization. An encouraging performance review invites the employee to evaluate the leader's performance and provides a chance for both worker and leader to discuss improvements in working and leading styles (see Appendix #12, Performance Review).

In an encouraging performance review, the employee finds out:

- How the manager evaluates his or her performance
- Where he or she stands with the manager

- What he or she can do to progress in pay and job status

- How secure his or her position is

Andrew Grove, CEO of Intel Corporation, characterized performance reviews "as the single most important form of task-relevant feedback which supervisors can provide employees. At Intel, we estimate that a supervisor probably spends five to eight hours on each employee's review, about one-quarter to one-third of one percent of the supervisor's work a year." He further notes that over the course of a year, "If the effort expended contributes to an employee's performance even to a small extent...isn't that a highly worthwhile expenditure of a supervisor's time?"[10]

Traditional performance reviews have lost their relevance. "The boss who plays God as an annual event doesn't sit very well with an empowered work force," says Julie Sackett, corporate vice president and director of personnel for Motorola's Government Electronics Group in Scottsdale, Arizona.[11]

Most performance management tools are retrospective; that is, they consist of hindsight. Such approaches look at how well an individual performed in the last year, six months, or other specific time interval. Most lab managers and supervisors detest this task. They procrastinate, and when they finally face up to it, they don't do a very good job.

Performance reviews should be regularly scheduled, starting with top personnel and proceeding throughout the organization. The philosophy is that people should review others in the way they would like to be reviewed themselves. The process if humane, simple, honest, and designed to improve relationships and performance. It should not involve extensive paperwork.

Performance reviews should be a two-way street. The leader might say, "I will tell you how I evaluate your work. Then I want you to tell me how I am doing as your supervisor."

Evaluations should be put in writing by executives, managers, supervisors, and all employees. Goals for the working relationship and work improvement should be established, with follow-up in two weeks or one month to determine whether both supervisors and employees are achieving their goals. The system emphasizes feedback that is specific, regular, planned, systematic, and encouraging. New hourly employees should be reviewed before the end of their 30- or 60-day probationary period.

The supervisor and the employee should evaluate their own performance before sharing evaluations of each other. Then they establish work improvement goals and set target dates and follow-up evaluation dates.

The process is designed to help the employee and the supervisor see themselves as they are perceived by their co-workers.

Performance review policy should include:

1. Frequency (usually twice a year)

2. Whether salary and promotion will be tied to the review

3. The amount of time to be spent on the review

4. Training sessions for managers on how to set achievable goals

In his best-selling book *Iacocca*,[12] Lee Iacocca makes a strong case for the *quarterly* review of subordinates. His logic for adopting such a time span is simple. The president of the company is required to make a quarterly report of results to the stockholders. Therefore, every manager should be required to make a quarterly report to his or her boss. Beyond that, the quarterly review system gives the leader a chance to make remedial changes in the qualitative and quantitative format of the organization.

Most people equate performance appraisals with salary review. The common perception is that the completed performance appraisal form is sent to the compensation department and used to determine salary increases. This view often results in managers manipulating performance data to achieve a certain salary recommendation.

In contrast, a much more beneficial use of the performance review places human resource development as its primary objective. When leaders view the performance appraisal as a significant tool that can help them improve their employees' performance, everyone benefits—the employee, the leader, the department, and the company. Guidelines to help reduce the anxiety that accompanies performance reviews and put the focus back on employee development are as follows:

1. ***Establish objective criteria for evaluation.*** Use mutually agreed upon goals, up-to-date job descriptions, and clearly stated standards of performance. This keeps the conversation focused on behaviors that have already been deemed most important.

2. ***Use lots of concrete examples.*** Note specific examples of the employee's successes as well as incidents that indicate a need for improvement. For example, instead of just saying, "You're a great communicator, but you need to work on follow-through," you might say, "I really liked the way you handled the meeting we had with the product manager and the folks from the packaging depart-

ment. You were very well prepared and kept the focus on the most important issues. Later, though, I noticed that some of the suggestions that were made in the meeting fell through the cracks." This raises a specific incident you can now discuss and from which you can draw conclusions.

3. ***Strategize together for future growth.*** After you have brought attention to the employee's specific areas of strength and weakness, brainstorm about ways to maximize the strengths and overcome the weaknesses. The discussion should include specific steps for getting there and a timetable.

   At all times, keep the meeting a discussion rather than a lecture, and make sure you are open to hearing and discussing the employee's point of view.[13]

4. ***Design feedback questions that reflect business goals.***

5. ***If staffers are expected to resolve conflicts without supervisory help, ask how the employee performs in this respect.***

6. ***Allow co-workers to answer questions anonymously.***

7. ***Add a bottom-up approach.*** The management information systems department at Pratt & Whitney, the aircraft engine manufacturer, created a Leadership Evaluation Improvement Process in which employees review supervisors. Employees anonymously answer a set of 19 questions to rate their supervisors in several categories, such as ability and willingness to communicate, leadership qualities, and team-building skills. A consultant compiles the responses and returns them to the supervisors, who then discuss them with their superiors.

8. ***Stay flexible.*** One of the main problems with traditional performance review systems is their rigidity. At many companies, they evolve into stacks of bureaucratic forms and deadlines that cannot be adapted to changing circumstances, and speed and flexibility are two strategic capabilities without which American companies cannot survive.

9. ***Set aside a block of time, and treat the review like any other important meeting.*** Block out at least 45 minutes. Do not put the review off by rescheduling; this is a significant event on your employee's calendar.

10. ***Meet in a conference room whenever possible.*** In addition to avoiding interruptions, the conference room is also a less threaten-

ing atmosphere. You are not behind your desk making pronouncements to your visitor. An employee who feels safe and relaxed is more likely to offer useful feedback and be more receptive to suggestions for improvement.

11. ***Treat the person as capable of change.*** The goal of most reviews is to improve things and not just enumerate problems like a list of criminal charges. One way to emphasize this is by referring to the desired improvements as things the employee is not doing yet.

12. ***Focus on specifics instead of numbers.*** De-emphasize any numerical scale used on the evaluation form. Discourage the employee from leaving your office as a "four." Point out that this is not a permanent assessment of the employee's abilities, but rather a current evaluation of how well he or she is putting them to use.

13. ***Observe body language.*** If an employee says that everything is just fine during the interview but is shaking his or her head, avoiding eye contact, or has both hands folded across his or her chest, the employee is probably not being honest with you. Point this out and begin again. Body language is an almost universally recognized form of communication. Consider saying something like, "Hazel, you say you agree, but I'm getting some very strong nonverbal signals to the contrary."

14. ***Spell out the next steps.*** How can the gap between current and expected behavior be closed? What could the employee do differently and when? Conclude the interview with a clear, explicit understanding of this. Ask the employee to restate what you have told him or her will happen next and what the ultimate goal is.

    In an ideal review, 60 percent of the time should be devoted to opportunities for improving the employee's performance. Although the term performance review seems to focus on past and present performance, what has happened since the last review is history. The emphasis should be on future performance, where the review can have a significant impact on productivity.[14]

15. ***To maximize the effectiveness of a performance review,*** it is essential to follow a format that will organize your approach to the review and guarantee that important questions are covered. The "3-P" approach—past performance, present performance, prospects for the future—helps facilitate this process. An important aspect of the "3-P" approach is its emphasis on future performance. If correctly implemented, the discussion of past and present per-

formance is less relevant than the concentration on promoting improved future performance.

Training in performance review methods needs to establish that:

1. Reviews are to be conducted with mutual respect.

2. There will be no hidden agendas. Reviews are not to be attacks or disrespectful.

3. Reviews are to encourage and improve performance.

4. Job descriptions and titles need to be established and clarified.

5. Performance review goals need to be fortified by daily supervision.

Digital Equipment Corporation uses a partnership approach to performance appraisals that includes both self and peer ratings. Typically, the annual appraisal includes input from every member of the employee's team. After receiving the input, a committee reviews it with the individual. The committee is usually made up of the individual, a chairperson who is usually an advocate of that individual's work, a management consultant, and two co-workers. For a performance appraisal to be successful, the individual's relationship with peers needs to be included.

There is little evidence to indicate that performance appraisals actually improve employee performance; however, even the toughest critics do not recommend abolishing them. One improvement might be to get management out of the loop. Toward this end, progress is being made in new work designs such as self-managed groups and high-involvement systems. Some of the faults of the traditional, rating-scale-based performance appraisal system can be attributed to human factors. Some bosses routinely manipulate the system to make it work for their own purposes. Some managers rate their employees artificially low in order to scare better performance out of them. To improve the accuracy of their appraisals, leaders should:

1. Listen well

2. Relinquish control

3. Approach negative information slowly and cautiously

4. Focus on observable behavior and give specific examples

5. Avoid arguments by refusing to put employees on the spot

6. Confront employees about performance deficiencies without inhibiting communication

Much of the stress associated with performance appraisals stems from failing to follow the practices that lead to effective appraisals. A survey of managers and their subordinates indicates that appraisals are ineffective when:

1. Performance standards are unclear

2. The manager lacks knowledge of actual work performance

3. The manager is not prepared for an appraisal

4. The manager lacks skills in conducting the appraisal

5. The appraisal is not taken seriously by the person doing the rating

Leaders can improve appraisal effectiveness by remembering that:

1. While rating forms are important, they are only part of the process

2. Appraisals must come from the top down

3. Appraisal training should be relevant to the situation

Managers need to be aware that performance appraisal can either solve or create problems and that employee improvement should be the focus of the appraisal.

Additional practical suggestions for making performance appraisals more encouraging than discouraging include:

1. Involve employees in the design of the performance management program

2. Make clear distinctions between the exceptional and the ordinary

3. Handle an employee failure with sensitivity so it does not become debilitating

4. Tie a large part of managers' own performance appraisals to how well they plan for, encourage, and assess the performance of their employees

5. Base performance decisions on results instead of personality

A Suggested Format for Performance Review

The following is a suggested format for beginning the process of performance appraisal. Such an interview should, of course, be supplemented by ratings based on an actual job description.

Name: _____   Self-Evaluation Date: _____

1. Current position (job description and expectations of employer and supervisor):_____

   _____

2. What is going well or has been accomplished? What do you take pride in? _____

   _____

3. What needs to be improved? _____

   _____

4. Supervisor Evaluation

   Strengths, assets, things going well:_____

   _____

   Things requiring improvement:_____

   _____

   Agreed-on plans for improvement: _____

   _____

5. Agreed-on achievable goals:_____

   _____

6. Supervisor's evaluation of employee: _____

   _____

7. Employee's evaluation of supervisor: _____

   _____

Dealing with Marginal Employees

One of the greatest areas of difficulty in performance appraisals is the manager's attitude toward the process and his or her willingness to make it work. The focus of the appraisal often strays from performance to personality. Fear of legal action on the part of employees is a major concern.

   Pfeiffer notes that too often managers do not deal effectively with problem employees because they want to avoid conflict. It is easier to ignore or deny the problem in the hope that it will disappear. However, the job of leaders is to benefit the organization and not to shield people from meeting performance standards. Three questions are helpful here:

1. Does the individual know that he or she is performing marginally?

2. How has the manager or organization justified the retention of the marginal employee?

3. What is the organization doing to reward productivity and excellence?[15]

"**F**eedback is the breakfast of champions."

Guidelines that Distinguish Encouraging Leaders

When conducting performance evaluations, consult the following guidelines:

1. Identify challenges and opportunities instead of problems.

2. Identify the positive potential in every person and every situation.

3. Be solution oriented.

4. Focus on strengths and manage weaknesses. Develop a leadership strategy to address weaknesses.

5. Remind people of their strengths.

6. Inventory assets and think of people in terms of their strengths.

7. Establish and align goals between the organization and the employee.

8. Appraise performance with positive performance reviews.

9. Explore choices and consequences.

10. Communicate openly and frequently.

11. Move away from a unilateral evaluation and have employees become more self-evaluative. Encourage employees to develop internal expectations and help them reach their dreams, hopes, and goals.

12. Spend considerable time *listening* to people. Hear the whole message.

13. Convey a positive, optimistic, "I know something good about you" attitude.

14. Make a conscious effort to point out what employees do right.

15. Help each employee appreciate the relevance of his or her contribution.

16. Treat everyone equally with regard to mutual respect and dignity.

17. See hidden assets and resources in your employees and spotlight them. Help reframe perceived negative shortcomings into positive strengths.

18. Give recognition for effort and improvement instead of just the finished task.

Phase 5: Consequences

Most employers have been in the position of trying to determine what to do with unproductive employees. They have searched for all kinds of remedial actions, often to little or no avail.

It is important to help an employee experience the reality of the situation. Consequences can be directly related to a failure to function. Examples of consequences of failure to perform may be no promotion, no raise or bonus, and no recognition in the company newsletter, memos, or on bulletin boards.

When implementing consequences, leaders must separate the deed from the doer. They need to be concerned with both present and future behavior instead of only the past. Consequences affect both the here and now and what will happen in the future.

Leaders should ensure that employees do not equate consequences with punishment. The term "consequences" implies that the employee is responsible enough to direct his or her choices and behavior and deal with the outcomes. A consequence may be addressed in a friendly manner that implies good intent.

1. Logical consequences—Result from the employee's performance. A variety of consequences are possible, each of which is selected as appropriate.

2. Encouragement—This is perhaps the most potent of all the motivational forces available to leaders. The encouraging leader is one who observes effort, movement, and any progress, however slight, an employee makes. The leader looks for *anything* positive that can be identified in the process the employee is implementing. Encouraging leaders are both respectful and enthusiastic about what they see happening to their employees. They are willing to work with employees so as to help them grow.

Encouraging leaders always can identify assets, strengths, potential, or resources in their employees. An encouraging leader is also able to see perspective and humor in a situation. The encouraging leader learns from mistakes.

Encouraging leaders regularly note the contributions of their employees and make certain that they and their co-workers are made aware of their progress.

3. Praise—Encouragement is not restricted to instances of outstanding performance or excellence. It can be given for the effort. Praise, on the other hand, recognizes exceptional performance. It notes the performance and comments on the excellence of the work. In praising, say what you specifically liked about the employee's behavior or accomplishment.

When superior performance is observed, do not delay in giving praise. Give the feedback as soon as possible.

When praising, respond to what the employee has accomplished instead of your expectation of his or her performance.

4. Reprimand—When an employee has made a mistake or has not functioned effectively, advise the person that he or she will receive some feedback in private. Then be specific about what was anticipated but is not happening. This type of feedback should be immediate, brief, and to the point.

Always confront the behavior and not the person. This might be done by using an "I" message (e.g., "When you do not reach your quota, I feel very disappointed because I thought we had agreed on how you could meet it."). This type of reprimand maintains an effective working relationship and clearly indicates that the person is valued even though his or her performance is not satisfactory.

Leaders need to understand how to approach a problem situation at work:

1. Identify the issue.

2. Clarify whether the problem is skill based or motivational.

3. Identify specific motivational components.

4. Identify what assets are available and how they can be related to established goals.

5. Appraise the performance in a clear, specific manner (see Appendix #6, The Encouraging Approach to Management).

An Encouraging Approach to Confrontation and Conflict

Respond to the following questions about how you approach conflict.

1. Conflict is:

2. When someone is in conflict with me I usually:

3. When I am in conflict with someone else I generally:

4. Briefly describe an incident involving conflict that you feel you were successful in resolving:

5. As you reflect upon that successful conflict resolution, what were some of the key strategies, attitudes, and/or behaviors that you utilized?

6. Now consider a past or current conflict. Briefly summarize the situation, including what has been done (if anything) to solve the problem.

We now present some theoretical and conceptual input. Later, you will be asked to revisit your conflict situation and consider new strategies.

Conflict is an almost inevitable aspect of leadership. The ability to problem solve in a conflict situation is an essential component of leadership by encouragement. Your basic approach to conflict is a first step in gaining greater awareness of your leadership style. Most of us have a "daily" style that we use when things are running well. For example, the Strength Deployment Inventory is an instrument that proposes three basic leadership styles. The "cool blue St. Bernard" is characterized by warmth, caring, empathy, and a strong focus on interpersonal relationships. The "hot red lion" is action oriented, focusing on strategies and solutions to problems. Conversely, the "analytical green fox" thinks about the situation, gathers data, and conceptualizes a hypothesis.

No one style is superior to another. Each style has various strengths and weaknesses, and many people use a combination of the three. There is often a "best-fit" approach that works better in different situations and with different personalities. Leaders need to be flexible enough to change strategies in different situations. Often, leaders change their basic style when there is a conflict as opposed to when things are going well. For example, co-author Eckstein tends to be predominately a "cool blue St. Bernard," with some "hot red lion." However, in cases of conflict, his style shifts to the "analytical green fox" who tries to figure out what is wrong. One disadvantage of such a shift in style is that he often becomes frozen or immobilized when in conflict until he can make sense of the situation. The benefit of such an approach is that it allows the psychologist part of him to utilize theories and models of human behavior in exploring underlying causes of or factors affecting the conflict. The strength of "red" is the emphasis on action, while a weakness would be like going forward with a play in a football game when a regrouping "time-out" is needed. A "blue" style is useful in considering the private logic or inner world of the other person but it may overlook technical components of the conflict.

Awareness of one's own style coupled with other problem-solving strategies is a first step in the leadership by encouragement approach to conflict. Review your response to question 5 above (successful strategies you utilized), and answer the following questions.

7. How would you characterize your style (blue, red, green, or a combination)?

8. If you were going to borrow or adopt some of the strengths you listed in question 5 to the challenge identified in question 6, what behaviors and/or attitudes would be necessary?

9. Suppose you were to shift your style and utilize another strategy, for example shift from "red" (action) to "blue" (relationships). How would you act differently?

An initial reaction to conflict is one of the "three D's": denial, delay, or diffusing the issue. Such avoidance strategies are often based on the hope that the situation will disappear or go away. In the 1970s, many Louisiana farmers were offered large sums of money to bury toxic waste containers on their land. They were assured that the steel-lined drums would safely contain the toxic waste. Over the years, however, the deadly chemicals ate through the steel drums and began seeping into the water supply.

Unresolved conflict is similar to buried toxic waste. While the conflict may appear to be safely contained, the "three D's" often result in a more costly future outbreak. Leaders who initially avoid the situation and allow it to build up run the risk of dealing with a stronger explosion than if the issue had been honestly addressed in the formative stages.

An encouraging approach to conflict also reframes the predominately negative connotations. For example, President John F. Kennedy was fond of noting that there are two Chinese symbols for the world crisis. The first is danger or troubled water, and the second is opportunity. Thus, just as a grain of sand motivates an oyster to form a pearl, so too is conflict a chance to do things differently, to improve the system, and/or to develop new relationships.

Suggestions for Constructive Conflict Resolution

The following sequence for conflict resolution was suggested by Herbert Kindler.[16] The process consists of four steps:

1. *Diagnosis*—Monitoring where differences initially exist in order to resolve the situation before it boils over into overt conflict. Potential sources of conflict are:

- Information is interpreted differently.
- Goals appears to be incompatible.
- Boundaries are violated.
- Old wounds have not healed.
- Symptoms are confused with underlying causes.

2. *Planning*—Developing a strategy and action plan.
   - Choose a strategy or a blend of strategies congruent with the situation, along with a backup plan.
   - Mutually agree with the other party on a time and place to explore differences and a time frame in which to do it.
   - Decide how to monitor the process and what the consequences of failure to live up to any agreement will be.

3. *Implementation*—Carry out the plan.
   - Maintain a tone of mutual respect and goodwill.
   - Consider putting any agreement in writing.

4. *Follow-up*—After agreement has been reached:
   - Monitor results to verify that the agreement is honored.
   - If the agreement is not being honored, learn why and then take corrective action.
   - Reinforce behavior that supports the agreement.
   - Learn from each experience with conflict and disagreement.

Now return once more to your original conflict situation and reflect on the following.

10. Given this additional theoretical information, what additional ideas do you have relative to your conflict challenge?

11. Finally, develop a series of action steps to implement a problem-solving strategy for your situation. Specifically, ask yourself what, who, and how you can encourage the representative participants (including yourself) in the situation.

The following items are meant to help you more fully identify your own "private logic" (filter) relative to the issue of confrontation.

Take a moment and write your spontaneous reactions to the word confrontation:

1. Make a list of words that describe confrontation:

2. Your major *feelings* about confrontation are:

3. Identify specific instances when you have needed to confront your workers.

4. Identify a time when you needed to confront an employee but avoided it.

Many leaders feel that confrontation is one of the most challenging aspects of their jobs. Conflict, unpleasantness, discomfort, and defensiveness are often associated with conflict, as is a knot in the pit of one's stomach.

A core concept relative to confrontation is *discrepancy*. Some specific examples include the discrepancy between:

1. What a worker's *job description* calls for contrasted with what he or she is actually *doing*

2. What a person says he or she is doing contrasted with what you or others *observe* being done

3. What a person *says* he or she will do contrasted with what is actually *being* done

The above examples are negative discrepancies in a worker's performance. However, it should be noted that the opposite is also common. One form of encouraging confrontation occurs when a worker's own disowned strengths result in a lower perceived standard of performance than the leader's estimation. Turning a perceived minus into a plus involves reframing or reinterpreting a specific action or attitude in a more positive manner.

For example, when one company implemented a new accounting procedure, one of the bookkeepers was excessively self-critical of her inability to learn the new system. "I appreciate how much effort you've put into learning the new system," her manager observed. "I also note your frustration and have heard you criticize yourself for being so slow to learn it. However, I want you to know that you are actually ahead of our projected timetable for changing over to the new system."

Even when an employee does need to be reprimanded, there are many different styles or approaches with which to confront. Too many leaders avoid a necessary confrontation because they associate it with a "battering ram" approach. Leaders need to learn other approaches to confrontation. A gentle, subtle approach often reduces defensive reactions when employees are striving to maintain their self-esteem.

Derogatory terms, sarcasm, and put-downs are ineffective approaches to confrontation. A more respectful approach confronts the discrepancy and still builds the employee's motivation. For example, "John, I felt our report could have been enhanced by the most recent sales figures. Is there any reason why I can't count on you to update those figures for next week's presentation?"

Not to confront a problem behavior or attitude is simply a form of denial or avoidance. Confrontation can and should be done in a respectful manner that clearly identifies the desired behavior. Separating the deed from the doer means pinpointing the specific issue in need of change and not engaging in a vague and undifferentiated attack. An example of positive confrontation is: "You are a valued member of our department. Your behavior of needs to be changed from...to..." Such an encouraging approach to confrontation is one of the distinguishing characteristics of leaders who are committed to excellence.

An Encouraging Approach to Firing

Firing should be the final problem-solving strategy after all other attempts at remediation have failed. Most terminations are due to irreconcilable differences in style (personal chemistry). In other words, the boss doesn't like the way the employee handles himself or herself. The majority of firings have very little to do with factors such as job performance, integrity, or insubordination—but they have a great deal to do with style! All too often, small adjustments in the organization or the individual would have solved the problem and salvaged a valuable employee.

*A **Firing Checklist**—*Before firing an employee, ask yourself the following questions:

- Am I angry? (Never act when you lose your temper.)

- Do I have all the facts?

- Did the employee know the rule and the disciplinary consequences of his or her conduct? If not, is it reasonable to expect that he or she should have known?

- Was the company's rule or my managerial order reasonably related in an orderly, efficient, and safe manner?

- Did I, before imposing discipline, make an effort to ascertain that the employee had indeed violated or disobeyed a rule or order of management?

- In the investigation, did management obtain evidence or proof that the employee was guilty as charged?

- Has the company applied its rules, orders, and penalties consistently to all employees?

- Does the punishment fit the crime? What was the company's past practice for similar misconduct?

- Where appropriate, has the employee been warned and given the opportunity to correct the problem?[17]

Firing is one of the challenges that can turn an entrepreneur into a manager, because it brings you face to face with failure. Nothing will make firing any easier. It shouldn't get easier. What it should become is less frequent. And that will happen if you make your company's firing process more instructive. If you think of firing as a symptom, or by-product, of your company's activities, then you can take responsibility for those failed employees. When you do that, you will understand why a company that hires the right people and manages them properly does almost no firing. That is the goal of an encouraging organization, and that is your ultimate goal: to hire and manage so well that you will never have to fire again. Here's how.

1. Hire right. Are you hiring the right people? Think about the people you have fired. What behavior ultimately made those people unsuccessful? Consider three broad categories: an employee's job aptitude, work attitude, and the proper fit with colleagues. Be specific.

Being comprehensive and thorough in your hiring procedures can also help you correct problems much faster if they do occur.

2. Make your expectations clear. The next biggest terminator of careers is failing to tell employees what you expect of them. The key is to give regular feedback to a new employee right from the start. Communicate your standards repeatedly and help employees understand what they need to change in order to succeed. Small companies cannot usually afford the luxury of a discrete orientation program, but they can, and often do, rely on a two- or three-week job rotation to teach new employees about the company and how it works.

3. Articulate why the person should be fired, and make sure the reasons are legal. A person may be dismissed for any reason not prohibited by law or by agreement between the parties. There is no legal requirement that a dismissal be fair.

Examples of reasons prohibited by law include:

- Dismissal because of race, sex, age, or religion
- Dismissal because of a disability

Elements of an agreement between employer and employee that may prohibit dismissal include clauses in individual employment contracts limiting the reasons for dismissal.

4. Make sure the reasons are supported by evidence. The type of evidence will depend on the reason for dismissal. The following are sample situations to illustrate the type of documentation usually needed.

If you are letting an employee go because of:

- *Poor performance*, you need documentation of instances of poor performance

- ***Misconduct***, you need documentation stemming from an investigation of the incident, including interviews with the employee and any other people involved

- ***No improvement*** in performance or behavior after repeated warnings, counseling, and opportunities to improve, you need documentation of these actions in notes to the file, memos of warnings, and evaluations

In some cases, there might be no prior documentation. While documentation of past discipline is desirable, it is not always necessary for a dismissal. Suppose, for example, that a staff member who has been a model employee for years one day gets into a screaming match on the phone with a customer. There is no legal reason why that person cannot be fired on the spot. The fact that there is no prior documentation does not make the firing illegal.[18]

5. Install early-warning systems. By the time most managers admit that something is amiss, it's late in the game. The nonperformer knows that something is wrong, and so do his or her co-workers. The manager chose to ignore the problem with the wayward worker until a drastic mistake was made.

6. *Fix the problems.* Evaluating what's wrong and changing it requires far more skill than anything else a manager does. No one can fix the problem but its owner—the weak performer. The manager acts as a facilitator by making the problem so crystal clear that the employee cannot resist fixing it.

7. *Explore other areas of the company where the employee might fit better.*

8. *Try to appreciate the employee's strengths and understand why your company couldn't harness them.* For example, say: "The last thing I wanted to do was put you in a position where you couldn't be successful. But I seem to have done that. Here are some of the problems we've had..." Scripting yourself is a good idea. By writing out your comments in advance, you can tailor your treatment to the individual.

9. *Make a serious effort to help the fired employee find another job.* Remember, if you really did your best in hiring the person, you believe in his or her basic qualities. You don't have to hire a costly outplacement firm to help the employee find another job. You can alert vendors, customers, and people in your industry and even provide a formal introduction in some cases. You can also make available some of your office's resources for a limited period of time.

10. Conduct an exit interview. What you hear in an exit interview could be the most candid, insightful criticism you will get. Hardly anyone conducts an exit interview after firing an employee, but it's worth the time. Assure the ex-employee that what he or she says will not cause you to withhold a good reference or other benefits you have already agreed upon.

11. Ask yourself what specifically was unacceptable about the fired person. How could you have predicted it in the hiring process? How could it have been corrected in the managing process? If you don't change anything after firing someone, then you are doomed to repeat the mistake.

Your firing experience could be the best instructor you ever have. A thorough analysis of a firing requires you to change your focus from solely your product or your market to managing human beings.

The number of wrongful termination suits filed over the last 20 years has skyrocketed by more than 2000 percent (compared with a 125 percent increase in overall civil cases in the same time period). Nearly 10 percent of the 2 million non-union and non-civil-service employees fired each year sue their employers. When employees do sue, they usually win. The average award is $500,000, but damages can soar into the millions.

Even when a company wins a suit, the costs are high. Lawyers' fees add tens of thousands—and sometimes hundreds of thousands—of dollars. A study of 120 wrongful termination suits in California conducted by the Rand Corporation, a research group based in Washington, D.C., revealed that legal fees and expenses can run as high as $650,000, with the average case costing $84,000.[19]

Avoiding Trouble

Here are some things to consider to reduce your chances of legal repercussions when you discharge someone:

1. Have an appeal policy. Such a policy should specify that no one in the company can terminate a subordinate without at least an opportunity for a hearing, appeal, or meeting with a higher authority.

2. Review your employee handbook, policy manual, and similar materials to eliminate any language that might be used as evi-

dence of an implied contract of continuous employment. For example, many policy manuals state that an employee will only be terminated for just cause.

3. Be sure that those who are involved in hiring and firing decisions avoid statements that imply employment as long as an employee performs well. If you have any kind of grievance procedure, be sure that it does not imply any right beyond "employment at will."

4. Develop and utilize a reasonable and practical performance review procedure.

5. Do not discharge any employee without a thorough, objective investigation into the facts of the case. It is best to start with a suspension and then move to dismissal after all the facts are known.

6. Be sure to get the employee's side of the story. Give him or her the opportunity to refute allegations of misconduct in front of witnesses. Keep detailed records of such discussions.

7. Consider writing general or specific disclaimers in your policy manual or employment application. A general disclaimer would, for example, explain how policy is made and who makes it and would point out that any commitment not made in accordance with such policy does not bind the company.

8. Some companies have written employment agreements that expressly include an "employment-at-will" understanding. Such an agreement is usually a signed contract stating that either party may terminate the relationship at any time with or without cause. This approach is only recommended for high-level executive, professional, or technical employees.

9. A handbook is a good idea, despite the fact that it can become a weapon in an unjust dismissal case. A handbook outlines the ground rules by which all employees must abide. It gives a perception of consistent treatment of all employees and serves as a guide for supervisory personnel.

10. Meticulous and accurate documentation is a cornerstone of all legally sound personnel practices. Document employee warnings, evaluations, and attendance and tardiness records. Also document all meetings at which career plans and promotions are discussed. Have the employee read and sign warnings and performance evaluations.[20]

11. Brief employees on their shortcomings before firing them. Unless the situation involves theft, destruction of property, drug use, or safety concerns, immediate dismissal is not a good idea. The initial warning should be delivered face to face, either at the annual review or at a special meeting.

    Have another supervisor or a member of the personnel department at the meeting as a witness, and let the employee know you take the problem seriously. Explain the problem clearly to the employee. Be firm, but don't condescend. For example, you might say, "We've had a client complain that you send your subordinates to meetings rather than go yourself. We pride ourselves on individualized service and think it's important that you be more attentive to this client's needs. Unless you address these complaints, we will have to reconsider whether you belong in this job."

12. Give employees a chance to correct problems. Warning employees and giving them an opportunity to improve will strengthen your case, since it shows that you have been fair and made the employee aware of your objections before the firing.

    Give the employee a reasonable time period in which to improve. The time frame should depend on the job and the seriousness of the problem. Whereas a secretary could show improvement in two weeks, a middle manager might need three months. Sometimes the nature of the problem dictates the appropriate time period. For example, if sales revenues were down in the employee's division during the first and second quarters, you might give her until the end of the year to improve.

13. Document verbal warnings. After each meeting with the employee, write a memo in which you clearly explain your concerns. For example, "Today I spoke to Jane Doe about the drop in division profits during the last three quarters. I told her that I expect profits to at least return to our original baseline level in the next quarter."

14. Follow up with a written warning. A written warning is evidence that the employee was told about the problem. The warning should be clear and direct. For example, "You will be fired if you continue to miss project deadlines." Avoid vague wording such as "If you fail to correct this problem, further action will be taken."

15. Watch your language. When you speak to the employee in person and in follow-up written warnings, be especially careful

not to say anything that could even loosely be interpreted as discriminatory.

16. Seek an independent review of the firing decision. Ask a third party to review all aspects of the case before you fire the employee. An objective evaluation may reveal underlying problems—and solutions. A reviewer might discover, for example, that a personality conflict is the source of trouble. Moving the employee to another area or department not only eliminates the possibility of a lawsuit but also saves the company the expense and time of hiring a new employee.

17. Be humane when you do the firing. Employees who feel they have been treated fairly are less likely to sue. Aim for a ten-minute, face-to-face meeting. Get to the point quickly. Tell the employee exactly why he or she is being fired: "Your performance in general has not been very good. Recent problems include your inability to meet deadlines, the decline in sales revenues in your division, and complaints from customers." Answer the employee's questions, but do not let the meeting drag on. If you are dealing with a question of fact, get the employee's side of the story and write it down. Creating an atmosphere of evenhandedness, if not compassion, goes a long way toward keeping an employee from feeling vengeful and seeking redress through the courts.

18. If you expect a problem, ask the employee to sign a release. If you think the employee will sue and are worried about your ability to defend the company's action, you may want to offer extra severance pay in exchange for a release from legal claims.

19. Do not hinder the employee's job search. Offer a generous severance package and outplacement help if possible. Good references can backfire, since they might suggest that there was no reason to fire the employee. Bad references can invite a libel suit, which you probably won't win. If prospective employers inquire, answer simply: "The company policy is merely to confirm the dates of employment. No inferences should be drawn positively or negatively with respect to the applicant."

The sooner the employee finds another job, the less likely he or she is to sue. A person who is not working has time to be angry about being fired and think about a lawsuit. An employee who has another job can put the firing behind him or her.[19]

"If you aren't fired with enthusiasm,
you will be fired with enthusiasm."

Vince Lombardi

SUMMARY

Following the improving management performance cycle creates a more "failure-free" work environment. The circular nature of the cycle implies that once all five phases have been addressed, the cycle begins anew with another issue.

This chapter provides a systematic procedure for increasing productivity. The process encourages by clearly identifying the real issue, which avoids the discouragement which occurs when criticism is not specific or relevant.

By identifying the assets, strengths, and resources of the individual, the leader recognizes the positive potential of the person. It is encouraging to receive feedback that points the way toward increased effectiveness. Clear, mutually agreed-upon goals are encouraging and motivating and create a feeling of involvement in one's destiny.

Performance appraisal is encouraging insofar as it provides feedback about the positive and ineffective elements of performance. Knowing how one's performance is evaluated is encouraging and gives direction to one's work.

Behavior and performance are directly related to the evaluation of effectiveness and productivity. Feedback that does not lead to clear consequences is confusing and discouraging. The improving management performance process provides for specific feedback and consequences leading to improved performance. Chapter 5 addresses more specific ways that leaders can be encouragers.

KEY POINTS

1. In a problem situation, identify whether the problem is due to skills or motivation.

2. Perceptual alternatives enable leaders to identify additional assets.

3. Goal alignment is the process of making the goals of the organization, management, and the worker consistent.

4. Consequences are an outcome or result of the employee's choices and behaviors.

5. The improving management performance cycle includes the following steps:
   A. Identify the issue
   B. Inventory the assets
   C. Goal setting and goal aligning
   D. Performance appraisal
   E. Consequences

LEADERSHIP BY ENCOURAGEMENT APPLICATIONS

This chapter provides a systematic model—the improving management performance cycle—for intervening in employee performance situations and turning them into opportunities to improve relationships and productivity.

Select a situation that is a challenge to your leadership and managerial skills. The situation can be any one that interests you and involves people. It can be at any level of management.

Take the steps outlined in this chapter and indicate your findings in written form. Identifying your progress as you go through the five steps is a good way to establish the improving management performance process as a systematic way of conceptualizing and resolving problems.

1. Develop answers for each of the five steps.

2. Share what you learned about yourself through the process.

3. Identify ways in which you can use the process in your work.

ENCOURAGEMENT SKILLS

Identifying the Issue

Whenever you face a challenge or problem as a leader, it is essential to step back and gain perspective on what the real issue is. Often the issue that appears on the surface (lack of manpower, materials, or cooperation) is not the underlying issue. If you work to correct the surface issue, you may have to continue to deal with similar problems in the future.

When a problem is presented, first identify whether the problem is due to lack of skill and ability or to a lack of motivation, involvement, confidence, or clear goals. The level of skill can be assessed by observing the employee performing the essential tasks. Some tasks lend themselves to objective measurement or feedback from clients, fellow workers, or supervisors. Lack of skill requires establishing the current level of skill and determining the type of training necessary.

Assessment of motivation requires greater awareness, sensitivity, and powers of observation. Your contacts with employees may help you to identify motivational problems. Lack of motivation requires discovering the employee's goals and interests and determining if the motivation can be increased or if the employee needs to be placed in a different position or replaced.

Lack of motivation in terms of cooperative effort and productivity can also be understood in terms of employee beliefs and priorities (see Chapter 3). If employees believe that life is unfair and no one can be trusted, they will not trust fellow workers or leaders. If their priorities are control and superiority, they will tend to challenge authority or may feel that too much is expected of them. In some instances, they will refuse to cooperate with workers who they do not consider to be at their level. If an employee has a belief or priority that works against cooperation, little change in the motivation area can occur until the real motives are dealt with. The following are some possible causes of motivational problems:

Result	*Possible Priority or Goal*
Challenges authority, wants to resist	*Need for control*
Feels inept, inadequate, or inferior	*Need for perfection*
Feels good at first, but then discouraged by need for approval or recognition	*Need to please*
Complains about how he or she is blamed for everything	*"Victim" attitude*

As you interview an employee, you may hear certain clues that reveal a pattern of thinking about self, others, work, and relationships. By ascertaining the employee's priorities and beliefs, you can identify the influences on interactions and behaviors at work. You can check your observations by sharing them in a tentative way with the employee. You might say, "I have an idea about what is causing a problem in your relationships at work. May I share it with you?" (obtaining permission and then providing your hypothesis tentatively). This does not trap the employee and makes it easier for him or her to consider the hypothesis honestly.

Vignette

Sue is an associate in the marketing department of a major publishing house. The accounts she has worked with have not been productive. In her last review, her supervisor indicated that Sue had poor feedback ratings. In her most recent interview, her supervisor indicated that it was clear that Sue did not have some of the basic marketing skills. When this was discussed, Sue became defensive and challenged her supervisor. Sue maintained that she was well-trained and that the real problem was inept associates and lack of help from her supervisor. The supervisor requested help in dealing with Sue.

1. Discuss the issues of skill and motivation in Sue's situation.

2. Describe how you would continue the interview with Sue.

3. What do you think the real issue might be?

4. Indicate how you came to that conclusion.

REFERENCES

1. Kern, R., *Lifestyle Scale*, Coral Springs, FL: CMTI Press, 1995.

2. Larsen, E. and Goodstein, J., *Who's Driving Your Bus: Codependent Business Behaviors of Workaholics, Perfectionists, Martyrs, Tap Dancers, Caretakers, and People Pleasers*, San Diego, CA: Pfeiffer & Company, 1993.

3. Hersey, P. and Blanchard, K., *Management of Organizational Behavior* (5th ed.), Englewood Cliffs, NJ: Prentice-Hall, 1988.

4. Field, L., *Skills Training for Tomorrow's Workforce*, San Diego: Pfeiffer & Company, 1994, pp. 33–41, 139–142.

5. Field, L., *Skills Training for Tomorrow's Workforce*, San Diego: Pfeiffer & Company, 1994, pp. 139–142.

6. Roseman, E., "Situational leadership, flexibility is the key." *Medical Laboratory Observer*, January 1983, p. 62.

7. Champy, J., *Reengineering Management,* New York: Harper Collins, 1995.

8. Pfeiffer, J., Goodstein, L., and Nolan, T., "Applied strategic planning." *The 1985 Annual: Developing Human Resources,* San Diego: Pfeiffer & Company, 1985.

9. Champy, J., *Reengineering Management,* New York: Harper Collins, 1995, pp. 161–162.

10. Davies, K., "Better performance from performance reviews." *National Management Association,* March 1990, p. 11.

11. Hubbart, W., "Make performance reviews meaningful." *Supervision,* August 1991, p. 26.

12. Iacocca, L., *Iacocca,* New York: Bantam Books, 1984.

13. Polsky, W., "How to give painless performance reviews." *Food Processing,* September 1993, p. 130.

14. "A twist on performance reviews." *Small Business Reports,* July 1993, p. 27.

15. Pfeiffer, J., "Encouraging managers to deal with marginal employees." *The 1984 Annual: Developing Human Resources,* San Diego: Pfeiffer & Company, 1984.

16. Kindler, H., "Managing conflict and disagreement constructively." *The 1995 Annual, Volume I: Training,* San Diego: Pfeiffer and Company, 1995, pp. 169–174.

17. James, R., "How to fire an employee legally." *Foundry Management and Technology,* March 1993, p. 50.

18. Webster, G., "How to fire an employee." *Association Management,* June 1993, p. 109.

19. Jacobs, D., "How to fire someone without getting sued." *Working Woman,* January 1990, p. 24

20. Sprigins, E., "How to fire." *Inc.,* May 1992, p. 67.

5

LEADERS AS ENCOURAGERS AND MOTIVATORS

"If you really want people to respond to your leadership, you have to have a personal relationship with them. They need to know you're dependable and that you'll be there if they have a problem. That's personal power to me."

Noreen Haffner

"The very essence of all power
lies in getting the other person to participate."

Harry Overstreet

INTRODUCTION

The role of the leader has changed dramatically. In the past, leaders often were selected because they were the most competent at performing specific tasks. However, just because an employee is knowledgeable and productive does not necessarily make him or her a good leader. In fact, promoting a technically competent worker to leader may result in double jeopardy—losing a good technical employee and creating an ineffective leader.

In the past, because leaders often were technical experts and could outperform everyone else in doing a particular task, it was assumed that their example would motivate others to become productive. Under these conditions, the authoritarian approach to management tended to be successful. Leaders knew more, were more skilled, and were more experienced; as a result, workers tended to accept and follow their directions. Power and action flowed from leader to employee. Leaders were seen as responsible for taking charge and controlling the organization, making decisions, and directing personnel. Management was concerned primarily with control and power. The belief was that by driving people, greater productivity could be obtained. Such authoritarianism worked in emergencies, but not in the long run.

Expectations of leaders changed after World War II. The significance of sales, marketing, and information grew, accompanied by rapid entry of the behavioral sciences into managerial training. As leaders began to realize that all people are not alike and that it is essential to recognize and accept individual differences, it became necessary to change the philosophy of management. The leader became the person who understood human nature and how to motivate individuals and organizations to become more productive.

As businesses grew more complex, the leader's role became more professional. Theories such as management by objectives and participative management became more important. Now, leaders are expected to understand and exhibit the characteristics of leaders. But there are discouraging leaders and there are encouraging leaders.

CHARACTERISTICS OF DISCOURAGING LEADERS

Domineering leaders alienate employees. Employees meet this authoritarian challenge with resistance and lack of cooperation. Authoritarian or dominating leaders often have good intentions but inappropriate methods. They usually refuse to tolerate mistakes or any type of imperfection. They do not admit personal weaknesses or allow them in employees. They believe that they are always right and know best. Their criticism, blame, and fault finding keep employees aware but anxious, confused, and less productive. Employees do not feel that they can trust the people they work for, enjoy the people they work with, or take pride in what they do.[1]

One of the goals of a leader is getting employees to perform as close to their potential as possible. A leader helps people become more effective by improving the quality of work life. At the same time, a leader is concerned with making his or her team highly productive and involved in the mission of the organization. Although this is obviously the purpose of management, some leaders are more concerned with power and control.

Power and control in any relationship stifle spontaneity, involvement, and cooperation. When power and control are emphasized, the potential of the employees is limited to incomplete involvement with the task. At times, management actually serves unwittingly as a discouraging element, and employees begin to think, "If the boss wants it done *his* way, let the boss do it himself."

Think about the most discouraging leader you ever experienced. Identify five traits this person exhibited that discouraged you.

The following are characteristics of a discouraging leader:

1. Never listens

2. Has double standards

3. Talks down to people

4. Belittles employees

5. Gives only negative feedback[2]

Sid Simon, a noted authority on values clarification, coined the phrase "red-pencil mentality" to identify managers who continually circle mistakes much like an English teacher grades a term paper.[3]

Some beliefs of leaders that interfere with employee motivation are:

1. I am responsible for everything and everyone.

2. I know more about everything than anyone else.

3. When I point out flaws and deficiencies, it motivates workers.

4. Perfection is expected; there is no need to recognize anything less. Why encourage people for what they are paid to do?

Sometimes unrealistically high standards for performance and productivity are established by leaders in an effort to raise productivity. However, such standards may have an unintended result. When workers begin to believe that there is no conceivable way to meet the standards of a critical supervisor, they give up and become passive participants in the company's business. Thus, high standards that were intended to raise involvement and productivity may actually produce the opposite effect. Pressure often results in hostility, theft, slow-downs, accidents, and poor workmanship.

For example, it has been estimated that more than half of stolen inventory in retail companies is taken by the employees.

Sometimes very ambitious leaders find that they are achieving exactly the opposite of their intended results. Overambition—the drive to be more, the push to move others to improve and to achieve—is often interpreted by employees as a sign that they are not good enough as they are. High expectations which constantly communicate to employees that they are not doing as much as they should be indicate lack of approval and appreciation, foster continual dissatisfaction with accomplishments, and resign employees to accept mediocrity.

In order to understand how to encourage, leaders need to understand some subtle methods of discouragement.

Subtle Methods of Discouragement

Discouragement Through Domination

Discouragement through domination occurs when leaders offer their strengths and talents to assist employees they perceive as ineffective. On the surface, the message is, "How can I help?" However, it is often received as, "I'll do that for you because I know you can't meet my standards." The supervisor has not prepared the worker to do the job. By stepping in and doing it for him or her, the leader teaches nothing but feelings of inferiority, dependence, and discouragement.

Leaders who dominate through intelligence and experience make their employees feel inept. The dominated person usually will display the following signs of discouragement:

- Inadequacy, not trying, or giving up

- Lack of self-confidence

- Feeling of unworthiness

- Tendency to avoid competition

- A belief that "If I wait long enough, the boss will take over."

In a relationship with a dominating person, one person is always inferior and the other is superior. Dominators usually speak as if they know it all. Those who receive this type of treatment often feel unable to stand up to the dominator. In such relationships, employees do not innovate or suggest improvements for fear of making mistakes.

"**I**f you pay in peanuts, expect to get monkeys."

Anonymous

Discouragement Through Insensitivity

Discouragement through insensitivity occurs when supervisors need to get even or gain power or are unaware of the needs of others. They attempt to increase their feelings of self-esteem and self-worth by controlling others.

In contrast, encouraging leaders are not fault finders; instead, they focus on strengths, assets, and potential. They have the ability to identify and encourage positive aspects. They give criticism privately and give encouragement and recognition publicly.

Discouragement Through Silence

Silence (the failure to comment) is a very subtle but effective way to alienate employees. The simple failure to notice an employee's efforts or contributions is a form of nonverbal rejection and communicates to the employee that his or her behavior is not what is expected or valued. When leaders fail to recognize employees' work efforts, they often discourage employees from continuing to invest energy in their jobs.

Many employees interpret silence as negative feedback. It has the same impact as criticism; it implies lack of acceptance. By failing to notice good work or progress, leaders essentially extinguish motivation and ignite discouragement.

When employees are appreciated and recognized, they develop energy for the task. Encouraging leaders increase employees' feelings of worth and self-confidence. As a leader provides positive recognition of employees, becomes acquainted with them, and calls them by name, employees develop confidence in their own abilities.

Discouragement Through Intimidation

Leaders may intimidate by treating people as objects instead of human beings. By judging only productivity and not appreciating the human factors, leaders intimidate individuals. Conversely, by considering people's goals, desires, and interests and working to develop their total involvement, leaders can improve productivity.

In some instances, the intimidation is the result of unrealistic standards of perfection. The message is that employees are not quite good enough and need to do more. The result is that employees come to believe that they cannot possibly meet such unrealistic expectations and in effect give up.

The Discouragement Process

We tend to think of leaders as motivators and encouragers. While leaders have responsibility for the total operation, they are responsible for getting employees involved and committed to common goals.

Such leaders function as delegators, trainers, educators, and encouragers. They provide leadership and motivation. They identify general, long-range responsibilities rather than specific, short-range tasks. Methods of achieving these goals are left up to the worker. Such leaders are typically more humanistic. They recognize their own limitations, are willing to admit their weaknesses, and admit that other people's opinions count, too. They get employees involved.

Motivating leaders focus less on blaming and fault finding and more on emphasizing strengths. They prepare people gradually and thoroughly for responsibilities at work. They are specific about what they expect and give credit for work done independently and effectively. Encouraging leaders give meaning and purpose to employees by recognizing and valuing their worth.

Successful leaders are more autonomous. They are in touch with their own feelings and are able to communicate them. Employees experience the motivating leader as someone who is supportive and concerned about them as people. They feel a personal relationship and connection.

Discouraged employees lack belief in their own abilities and tend to see life and work as unfair. They show up for work and put in their time but essentially only go through the motions. They see little purpose to their employment beyond receiving a paycheck. These employees do not experience a feeling of involvement with the organization and its goals of service and productivity. It is evident that such employees reduce the effectiveness of the organization. Their lack of involvement, belonging, and participation results in a discouraging work experience for both the leader and the employees. Their negative attitude is contagious and spreads throughout the team.

It is important to understand the dynamics involved in the discouragement process. It is not unusual to assume that competition, fear, and the threat of being fired will enhance productivity. In fact, they usually produce exactly the opposite. In a highly competitive atmosphere, people often feel uncertain about their own adequacy and their place in the organization. As they come to doubt their own value and their feelings of inferiority increase, they become discouraged about their ability to make progress.

When workers are not respected and treated with dignity, they often feel overcontrolled, rebellious, insecure, and helpless. This discouraging atmosphere reduces their motivation, involvement, and commitment to the company.

In order for employees to develop self-esteem and feel that they are capable, involved, and important, they have to feel valued. Feeling valued fosters a desire to participate enthusiastically in accomplishing the company's goals.

> "The president of our company says he's surrounded
> by "yes men." He told me so himself, and I agreed with him."
>
> Anonymous

Employees frequently complain that the boss neither knows them nor cares about what they are doing; they are only numbers. As an organization grows, it becomes increasingly important to personalize the way employees are treated, give them a sense of belonging to the organization, and involve them in planning and decision making.

> "I have yet to find a man, however exalted his station, who did not
> do better work and put forth greater effort under a spirit of approval
> than under a spirit of criticism."
>
> Charles Schwab

There are alternatives to autocratic management. Today, we conceive of leaders as *encouragers* and *motivators*. In addition to their organizational responsibilities, leaders are concerned with getting employees involved and committed to mutually agreed-upon goals.

CHARACTERISTICS OF ENCOURAGING LEADERS

Many personality theorists believe that encouragement is the basic change agent for all human behavior. Most people have experienced encouraging and discouraging leadership. To help conceptualize the contrast, think about the most encouraging leader you have ever experienced. Identify at least five traits this leader exhibited that encouraged you.

The following are characteristics of an encouraging leader:

1. Really listens to employees

2. Respects employees' abilities and believes in them

3. Is enthusiastic

4. Has a sense of humor

5. Admits his or her mistakes

6. Gives employees credit for their ideas

7. Is positive[2]

> "Just being available and attentive is a great way to use listening as a management tool. Some employees will come in, talk for twenty minutes, and leave having solved their problem entirely by themselves."
>
> Nicholas Iuppa

Encouragement focuses on the positive and creatively, consistently seeks ways to reframe limitations as potential assets. It is obvious that the person who encourages not only improves the working relationship but also helps motivate the worker.

Successful leaders are more autonomous. They are in touch with their own feelings and are able to communicate them. Encouraging leaders also recognize their own limitations, are willing to admit their weaknesses, and admit that other people's opinions count. They get employees involved.

Such leaders function as delegators, coaches, trainers, educators, and encouragers. They provide leadership and motivation. They assign general, long-range responsibilities rather than specific, short-range tasks. Methods of achieving goals are left up to the workers.

Effective leaders understand what motivates employees. Employees like to feel that:

1. They are involved in a relationship with their leader and are more than numbers or objects

2. They are connected with and belong to a community with common goals and concerns

3. There is mutual respect and trust

4. They are fully vested in the success of the team, department, and organization

5. Managers care and are available when support is needed

6. Specific goals provide clear direction

7. Their opinions are respected and considered

8. Their ideas are recognized and rewarded

Effective leaders recognize effort and contributions. They send positive memos, with copies to the boss. They visualize each employee as holding a sign that says, "Make me feel important; let me know that I count."

When encouragement is part of daily supervision, less time is spent emphasizing mistakes, deficits, and imperfections. Mistakes are recognized and discussed, but what was *learned* from the experience is emphasized.

For example, Joe's new secretary, Laura, is trying hard to meet the requirements of the job. In the process, she decides to save money by using regular mail instead of express mail. Much confusion results because paperwork is not delivered on time. Instead of blaming Laura, Joe tells her that he knows she is embarrassed and simply asks her to fax the paperwork to the person expecting it. The tension is alleviated, and Laura's performance is corrected.

Building Employee Self-Esteem

The ability to identify resources and to see a diamond in the rough is essential in the encouragement process. The leader sees the talent in an individual and communicates the positive so that the person realizes his or her own possibilities. The leader goes beyond limitations and present capabilities by visualizing potential. The employee then has a chance to reach his or her potential in the workplace.

In order for employees to develop self-esteem and feel that they are capable, involved, and important, they have to feel valued. Feeling valued fosters a desire to participate enthusiastically in accomplishing the company's goals. Encouraging leaders approach employees with positive expectations and, as a result, get maximum performance. Encouraging leaders are usually enthusiastic. They have confidence in themselves, their plans, and their colleagues. As a result, those who work with them tend to feel surer of themselves and are more willing to become involved.

Encouragement helps employees to believe in their abilities and increases their self-confidence. Employees are encouraged to accept and learn from all their experiences. They learn that mistakes are not disasters but learning opportunities. They change the focus from perfectionism, which reduces productivity, to achievement through the courage to be imperfect. They are motivated to give their best effort and cooperate because they know their contributions are valued.

Motivating leaders focus less on blaming and fault finding and more on emphasizing strengths. They prepare people gradually and thoroughly for responsibilities at work. They are specific about what they expect and give credit for work done independently and effectively. Encouraging leaders give meaning and purpose to employees by recognizing and valuing their worth.

> "Catch someone doing something right."
>
> Kenneth Blanchard and Spencer Johnson

Seeing in Perspective

Our experiences—whether positive or negative, inspiring or discouraging, successful or not—are influenced by our perspective, or the way we see things. Our point of view about ourselves, our work, and human relationships influences how we meet the challenges of life.

How we perceive situations affects our courage, decisiveness, and effectiveness. Expectations are a major influence on success in meeting challenges. If we expect that another person will be very difficult to relate to, or if we anticipate that a situation is beyond our ability, we will probably be less successful than if we are able to put the person or situation in perspective and recognize that we may be exaggerating the problem.

We are often discouraged as a result of our self-constricting perceptions, private logic, and restricting beliefs, which reduce our field of vision. If we believe that other people are more capable, we limit ourselves in all situations. Limited, discouraging perceptions place us at a disadvantage.

The encouraged person has a broader perspective and is able to develop new and unlimited vantage points. He or she is able to see both sides of a situation and his or her ability to consider possible solutions is not constricted.

Our ability to see in perspective is greatly enhanced by our self-esteem and self-confidence and by recognizing our own strengths and resources. When we see how our resources can be used, our enthusiasm is stimulated. When our perspective is wider, we see possibilities and recognize options. We feel empowered to make choices and decisions.

"**A**ttitude change will be enhanced if the recipient
of the message participates in the process of persuasion."

K. Shaver

Reduced participation in any organization stems from employees feeling that what they do makes no difference. As a result, leaders may encounter some of the following difficult personalities:

1. *Employees who demand to be noticed (attention-getters)*— They are not team players and are not concerned with the progress of the entire organization. They spend most of their time concentrating on their own progress or putting others down. They are competitive and more interested in themselves and the benefits they derive than in connecting with fellow employees.

2. *Employees who seek power by challenging authority*—Their game is to prove themselves right and the leader wrong. The boss frequently reacts to such people with anger because of their lack of cooperation. Unions often pick as leaders power-oriented individuals whom management has underutilized. These leaders tend to be in opposition to company policies. Such leaders can become enthusiastic about management goals if they are appreciated, understood, utilized, and included in decisions that affect employees.

3. *Individuals who feel that the organization has treated them unfairly*—These individuals focus on revenge. They are concerned with getting even for not being promoted, receiving a low raise, or any other form of perceived mistreatment. They challenge leaders to make them care.

4. *Discouraged employees*—These individuals display ineptness or inadequacy in performing a task in order to be excused from participating.

   To illustrate, suppose it is five o'clock on a Friday afternoon and a leader needs to ship a last-minute package. She goes to the shipping department, but everyone has left for the weekend. While returning to her office, she runs into a clerk from the data processing department and asks him to help her out. Although the task is not part of the clerk's job description, the leader knows that the task is something the employee can do well. When forced to do the job, the employee does it so poorly that the leader has to look for someone else to help ship the package. Thus, by displaying ineptness and inadequacy, the employee is excused from functioning.

Determining What to Focus On: Looking at the Relationship

It is important to understand the beliefs, attitudes, and goals that are part of a person's self-defeating behavior.

Any communication includes ideas, feelings, beliefs, and goals. These are all routes to understanding human behavior. A leader who is not skilled in listening tends to respond primarily to the content or one facet of the message. A focused listener hears the whole message, both verbal and nonverbal, and decides how to respond. Perceptive and sensitive listening results in a response that communicates understanding. To lead, one must listen. For example:

> *Bill (leader):* "Your shift is constantly failing to produce what I need."

> *Joe (supervisor):* "I'm doing the best I can. Your standards and expectations are too high. Purchasing held us up on parts twice this week, we had a machine breakdown, and three set-up men took the week off to go hunting. I can only do so much."

If Bill chooses not to listen to Joe, he might say, "Excuses will not solve the problem; results will." On the other hand, if Bill chooses to listen to Joe, he might respond by saying, "Why do you say my expectations are too high? What will help solve the purchasing and attendance problems?"

The effective leader hears the other person's point of view and pinpoints the real issues. Making a joint decision about change improves the situation. However, being repeatedly discouraged also has a purpose; there is a payoff in not taking a risk and in not trying to solve the problem. The supervisor above may need long discussions with the leader to reinforce his own problem-solving abilities.

Workers need to face their own self-defeating behaviors and be aware of how such behaviors keep them from reaching their potential. Overcoming habitual self-defeating beliefs and behaviors is a major challenge. Establishing an atmosphere that encourages open discussion and allows mistakes is a first step.

The encouraging leader recognizes any effort on the part of discouraged employees to change. The effort itself represents movement and progress. The encouraging leader needs to be there at the moment of effort, observe it, recognize it, and verbalize it.

When discouraged workers have encouraging leaders who believe in them, recognize their progress, and do not judge them, they are more likely to take risks and eventually take effective action.

Employees experience the motivating leader as someone who is supportive and concerned about them as people. They feel a personal relationship and a connection.

A SYSTEMATIC PLAN FOR
LEADERSHIP BY ENCOURAGEMENT

An encouraging organization does not happen by chance. It is the result of clear objectives, planning, and a philosophy of getting maximum involvement from people through positive managerial attitudes. Consistent encouragement begins with the top executive. Trust is spread by educating every leader in how to motivate people at work.

The top executive of an organization needs to share the organization's mission and long-range goals through training programs, staff meetings, publications, and company-wide meetings. The comptroller needs to share trends in costs, prices, cost reductions, and taxes. The chief engineer needs to communicate progress in and roadblocks to getting new designs completed. Manufacturing needs to keep everyone aware of delivery dates, equipment needs, and maintenance problems. Purchasing needs to inform others about supplies, new materials, deliveries that influence customer delivery dates, etc. Personnel needs to inform everyone about job openings, payroll policies, union grievances, promotions, and shift changes and encourage workers to report any human relations problems.

Encouraging leaders establish formal communication systems up and down the line through staff meetings, memos, company newsletters, bulletin boards, union–management meetings, continuing education courses, and ad hoc committees.

Encouraging leaders clearly demonstrate that the company belongs to everyone. They are not afraid to credit employees and to show appreciation, both verbally and nonverbally. As Cox indicated, encouragement is the art of empowerment. "Encouragement needs to flow in four directions: up, down, across, and inward."[4]

Leaders are encouraging when they cooperatively identify performance targets for employees. They analyze situations and determine what went right as well as what went wrong. They have the courage to be imperfect, critique their own management decisions, and learn from failures and mistakes.

Encouraging leaders try to move away from an evaluative role and encourage and teach their employees to become more self-evaluative. They are less concerned about finding fault and placing blame. They emphasize cooperation, sharing information, and personal empowerment and responsibility. There is movement toward a relationship that is horizontal, in which people deal with one another as equals even though they may have different titles, functions, and salaries. As employees begin to feel valued and respected, they have more energy for involvement with the organization.

In order for leaders to plan an encouraging approach, they need to ascertain the goals of individual employees: what they would like to happen in their jobs, how their jobs could become more meaningful to them, what they want to happen in their careers in the next year or five years, and so on. After determining the goals of their employees, leaders can find ways to align those goals with the goals of the organization.

As leaders start to creatively fit specific goals of employees with organizational goals, they will find an increase in involvement, productivity, and participation. By working with employee goals, the process is energized.

When leaders work against the goals of the employees, mischief, lack of cooperation, and lack of participation in the organization's goals are often stimulated.

Behaviors That Encourage

1. Spend a great deal of time listening to people. When people feel the stress of too much to do, often they are tempted to give quick answers, whether they are appropriate or not. Focusing on what people are communicating—their beliefs, feelings, and motives—creates understanding and helps them feel accepted.

The legendary Dale Carnegie describes meeting a distinguished botanist at a dinner party given by a New York publisher. He became enthralled with the botanist, literally sitting for hours listening to his descriptions of exotic plants and indoor and outdoor gardens. At the end of the evening as the botanist was leaving, he told his host many positive things about his experience with Carnegie, concluding with the observation that Dale was a "great conversationalist." This compliment caused Carnegie to ponder, "I had said hardly anything at all...I had done this: I had listened intently. I had listened because I was genuinely interested. And he felt it. Naturally that pleased him. That kind of listening is one of the highest compliments we can pay anyone. And so I had him thinking of me as a good conversationalist when in reality I had been merely a good listener and had encouraged him to talk."[5]

Andres Navarro, president of SONDA, S.A., a South American computer systems company, uses the Spanish language to differentiate between hearing and listening. "In Spanish," Navarro explains, "we have two words, *oir* and *escuchar,* the rough equivalent of 'to hear' and 'to listen.' To really listen is much more than just hearing. Many people, when they are hearing someone, they are really thinking to themselves 'what will I answer?' instead of trying to listen to what the person is saying."[6]

2. Have a positive, optimistic attitude about the work and the people. Beginning one's work or contact with people with a positive and optimistic orientation facilitates growth and development.

3. Make a conscious effort to point out the things that employees do right instead of just their mistakes. Leaders used to believe that focusing on mistakes improves performance. Experience and research indicate that recognizing any effort or positive movement increases productivity.

4. Believe that each employee needs to know how meaningful his or her contribution is. The more people feel that their work has meaning and their contributions are valued, the more they tend to be involved and committed.

5. Whenever possible, involve employees in decisions about how you can most effectively achieve the goals of the organization. The more people are involved in meaningful decision making, the greater the probability they will devote increased effort to reaching organizational goals.

6. Show genuine interest in employees and their welfare and have a good understanding of each person's long-term goals. Bill Makahilahila, vice president of SGS Thompson, describes the Human Resource Quality Award, a program that recognizes employees for excellence in human relations. The program includes the Golden Ear Award for good listening, the Silver Tongue Award for good communicating, the Empowerment Award, and the People Leadership Award for an outstanding display of honesty, integrity, and sincerity.

7. Be open-minded toward employees' ideas. Mary Kay Ash, the cosmetics company founder, describes an influential moment in her career. After borrowing twelve dollars from friends to attend her first Stanley Brush convention, she recalls three key items from the keynote address. "First, get a railroad to run on. Then hitch your wagon to a star. Finally, they said, tell someone what you're going to do." At the conclusion of the talk, she boldly marched up front and informed Mr. Frank Sammy Beverage, the CEO, that next year she would be crowned queen, as had happened to another woman that evening.

Mary Kay smiles and adds, "Now, if he knew who he was talking to he would have laughed. I was three weeks in the business, seven dollar Stanley party average, and I was going to be queen next year? Come on now, really. But he was a very kind man. I don't know what he saw in me, but he took my hand, looked me straight in the eye and said, 'You know, somehow I think you will...'" Mary Kay continues, "These seven words changed my life. I couldn't let him down. I mean I had pledged that I would be queen next year." And she was![6]

8. Solicit new ideas from people regularly. Believe in the value of employees' ideas. When employees do not share ideas about what they would like to see improved, it usually indicates lack of trust. Ways to solicit employee suggestions include a suggestion box, open meetings for all employees, brainstorming sessions, and an open-door policy.

9. Don't view mistakes as catastrophes. Simply correct mistakes and set up a system to minimize the chances of recurrence. View mistakes as learning opportunities. When they occur, help employees to analyze what went wrong and what they can learn. The focus should not be on placing blame. When people who have made mistakes are treated respectfully, not only will they not make the same mistakes again, but they will feel respected, trusted, and involved.

10. Listen to new employees' feelings about the job, provide a safe atmosphere in which they can ask questions, and introduce them to each staff member. A company functions best as a family or team. Personally welcome new employees and introduce them to the people with whom they will be working. This relatively small investment of time is a primary process in team building and helps new employees to feel valued, important, and that they belong.

11. Be sensitive to the feelings of people who have been away from work. People who have been away from work need to be kept informed of what has transpired. When they return, have a member of their department spend some time sharing major developments and changes that occurred while they were gone.

12. Encourage employees to trust you. Trust is fostered by trusting others. A leader communicates faith in employees by involving them in decisions.

13. When confronting employees, tell them very specifically why they are being confronted and exactly what you expect from them. Then express your belief that they can improve. When an employee makes a mistake, explain the problem in a nonblaming manner. If the mistake reoccurs, consider temporarily relieving the employee of that responsibility and providing additional training. Be sure to check back on the employee's progress.

14. Be a positive team leader who communicates "we can do it." Enthusiasm and energy communicate that the leader is with the team and that he or she knows the team will succeed.

15. Treat everyone equally. Encouragement is communicated clearly when there are no favorites, privileges, or special rules and when all employees are treated with equal respect.

16. Confront discouraged, unproductive people in private. Discipline is best done in private. Avoid embarrassing the employee and making the problem public.

17. Have confidence that with proper training, your employees can do the work. Delegate responsibilities. Delegation is one of the most effective ways to encourage and communicate faith in employees. Be clear about what is being delegated, when the task is to be completed, and how it will be evaluated.

18. Develop an ability to see hidden assets and resources in your employees. The encouraging leader focuses on strengths, resources, effectiveness, potential, and possibilities. Identify and encourage what is not always apparent even to the employee.

19. Focus on mutual cooperation, rather than competition, to build team power. Dale Carnegie relates a relevant incident reported to him by Charles Schwab, the millionaire steel executive. One day at lunchtime, Schwab was walking through one of the steel mills when he came across a group of men smoking directly under a no smoking sign. Rather than confront them about their rule violation, he simply stopped and chatted with them in a friendly manner. As he was leaving, he handed them some cigars, smiled, and said, "I'd appreciate it, boys, if you'd smoke these outside."[6]

Contributing, collaborating, and commitment to team goals are more effective than competition. The sense of belonging, being part of a team, and making a valuable contribution is powerful.

20. Give recognition for effort and improvement instead of only the finished task. Progress, growth, and productivity are the result of carefully, intentionally recognizing any attempt, effort, improvement, or movement in a positive direction. Recognizing the effort fosters motivation, courage, and increased enthusiasm.

Developing an Encouraging System

The following are some fundamentals for developing an encouraging system:

1. Establish mutual organizational and personal goals for workers. Resistance to cooperation indicates lack of goal alignment. Encouraging leaders help employees develop and express their goals and find effective ways to reach them.

2. Create an attitude of belonging that communicates "This is our organization; we produce this product or service and we are proud of what we are doing." Profit-sharing, for example, fortifies this sense of responsibility. In many companies, every employee is a stockholder.

3. Create an atmosphere of pride in ownership and craftsmanship. Provide the necessary training. Recognize progress and achievement.

4. Involve employees in decisions related to the business and in planning for the organization. Develop a procedure for participation in management. Involve all employees meaningfully and regularly through weekly team meetings, open communication, an open-door policy, and company-wide meetings. According to Plunkett and Fournier, "In our view, participative management is a philosophy that demands organizational decision-making be made in such a way that input and responsibility are extended to the lowest level appropriate to the decision-making made. The purpose of participative management is to ensure that effective decisions are made by the right people."[7]

5. Recognize and appreciate all kinds of contributions or positive movement. Creativity and energy are released when the company assigns people so that they can use their strengths. The education, training, experience, talent, and interest of every employee need to be known and utilized (see Appendix #14, Asset Focusing).

"**R**ecognition drives the human engine."
Leonard Berry, Texas A&M University

CREATING THE ATMOSPHERE TO IMPLEMENT ENCOURAGEMENT

The encouraging leader–employee relationship is based on mutual respect and openness. When problems arise in relationships, communication is based on nonevaluative listening. Each party is interested in hearing the facts as well as the feelings, beliefs, intentions, and attitudes of the other. Discussions focus on change as opposed to argument or confrontation.

Such a relationship is based on a belief that each person is worthy of respect. Instead of blaming each other, the leader and the employee are empathic in a sincere effort to overcome the roadblock together.

> "**R**emember that when an employee enters your office
> he is in a strange land."
> Erwin Shell

ENCOURAGING SELF-EVALUATION

Initiative is stimulated when employees do not fear external evaluation and focus on internal evaluation. The ultimate responsibility for personal growth lies with each individual; outside pressure only shifts the responsibility. As employees develop the capacity to evaluate their own behaviors, decisions, and progress, they develop the courage to try to clarify their goals. When the goals have been developed mutually by the employee and the leader, specific methods of evaluation are also established (see Appendix #5, Evaluating Your Leadership Relationships, and #4, Assessing Encouraging Leaders).

Self-encouraged employees are able to:

1. Take responsibility for their own work and the work of their teams

2. Trust their own judgment

3. Become independent of external evaluations

4. Openly receive honest feedback about job performance and their relationship with the manager

5. Show less dysfunctional behaviors, such as seeking attention or power, revenge, apathy, or an inability to function effectively

6. Take risks and show courage in trying new experiences, ideas, processes, etc.

7. Be open and honest about their feelings, beliefs, and actions

The leader's goal is to help employees learn to trust and accept themselves, become more involved, and eventually be more productive. This evolves as employees develop the ability to evaluate and encourage themselves, which is a major step toward personal maturity and self-motivation.

FOCUSING ON EFFORT AND CONTRIBUTIONS

To motivate greater involvement and productivity, the leader needs to focus on increasing people's feelings of worth and belonging. Focusing on effort contrasts with focusing on completed projects and outstanding work. While the eventual goal is developing self-motivated workers who creatively face any challenge, with many people that is best reached by recognizing their efforts and progress toward the final goal.

The ability to focus on effort is enhanced by a positive, long-range view of an employee's development. Focusing on effort and contributions requires tuning in to even small indicators of positive movement or increased energy, interest, or enthusiasm toward the activity or project. See the potential and guide the individual toward greater satisfaction by primarily commenting on effort and progress. People are usually aware of their mistakes and do not need you to emphasize them. When people do not recognize their mistakes, you should help them become aware of changes that are needed while at the same time focusing on any progress they have made. If someone is experiencing difficulty in one part of the job, remind him or her of positive progress in other parts of the job.

Your focus needs to be, "I can always see the positive possibility in any situation." As people come to anticipate that you are supportive and encouraging, they become free to use their potential.

Vignette

Your new secretary is very effective in taking dictation and typing your correspondence. However, in her haste to be efficient, from time to time she mails things incorrectly, which creates confusion.

Your secretary is also very effective in communicating positively on the telephone. At times, however, she gets names and messages confused, and when you follow up, you sometimes find yourself in an embarrassing position.

You identify the problem not as lack of ability, but as her trying to accomplish too much and being overly concerned with the quantity of her work rather than with accuracy. In talking with your secretary, begin by discussing what you like about the work she is doing for you.

1. What are some efforts and contributions you could focus on?

2. How can you be most effective in encouraging her?

3. What would be the most effective way to deal with the errors?

SUMMARY

Effective leaders are aware of the encouraging and discouraging elements of the leader–associate relationship. They avoid unrealistically high standards, domination, and insensitivity. They clarify employee goals that are aligned with organizational goals. They establish a systematic plan for encouragement.

In an encouraging system, employees feel that they can participate and that they belong.

KEY POINTS

1. Power, control, fear, and punishment stifle spontaneity, involvement, and cooperation and reduce productivity.

2. Discouragement can occur as a result of domination, insensitivity, silence, and intimidation.

3. Leaders are more effective as encouragers and motivators than as controllers.

4. Good leaders are able to communicate their true feelings and admit their mistakes.

5. Employees need to feel involved and appreciated.

6. Encouragement involves focusing on an individual's assets and resources.

7. Encouraging leaders recognize and point out an employee's strengths and assets.

8. Encouraging leaders identify potential resources.

9. Encouraging leaders recognize positive effort and improvement.

10. Encouraging leaders build employee self-esteem.

11. Expectations are powerful motivators.

12. Encouraging leaders understand the purposes of resistant be- haviors.

13. Encouraging leaders know the goals of each of their employees.

14. Encouraging leaders have positive expectations and are confident and enthusiastic.

15. Encouragement is most effective when it is done systematically throughout the organization.

16. Encouraging leaders develop a system that encourages self- evaluation and self-encouragement.

LEADERSHIP BY ENCOURAGEMENT APPLICATIONS

Discouragement is a powerful obstacle to the development of enthusiasm, energy, and involvement.

1. Identify some of the subtle ways that your company's culture discourages employees.

2. List some of the ways you may discourage others in a subtle, but unintentional, manner.

3. What have you learned about yourself and discouragement? How will you begin to move away from being discouraging?

4. Encouragement is a powerful motivational philosophy and tool. What are some significant ways in which you can be more encour- aging and:

   A. Change the atmosphere in your company

   B. Work with specific individuals to improve your relationship with them

You as an Encouraging Leader

Are you the kind of manager who can honestly and effectively use encouragement? To develop some awareness about yourself and your approach to relationships and management, take the following test and evaluate yourself.

Place an X in the column that best describes your current actions, attitudes, and feelings.

	Definitely	Sometimes	Seldom
1. I believe that it is my responsibility to help develop my subordinates.			
2. I have a plan for identifying the positive in every person.			
3. I am an attentive listener.			
4. I respond to the feelings of my employees in an empathic way.			
5. I hear my employees' messages and clearly indicate what I hear.			
6. I can put my employees' feelings and thoughts into words so they feel understood.			
7. I respect my employees' ideas even though I may not think they are as good as my own.			
8. I understand my employees' concerns and communicate that understanding to them.			
9. I am enthusiastic when I recognize and respond to my employees.			
10. I focus on my employees' strengths and resources.			

	Definitely	Sometimes	Seldom
11. I find alternatives for solving problems presented to me.			
12. I recognize and focus on enthusiasm, effort, and participation.			
13. I take a positive attitude on most issues.			
14. I encourage my employees to participate in the managerial process.			
15. I provide honest and open feedback.			
16. I give credit when it is due.			

Go back through the test and evaluate your responses as follows: definitely = 3 points, sometimes = 2 points, seldom = 1 point. If you scored 33 points or higher, you probably have the attitudes of an encouraging manager.

ENCOURAGEMENT SKILLS

Vignette

Jack owns a business that sells specialized insurance nationwide. When it is time to collect payment on a policy or there is a new client to be seen, Jack believes it is his responsibility to make the call and handle the details. He does not believe that his associates can handle these situations. He is concerned that they will offend clients or lose new business. His associates handle only minor accounts.

1. What are Jack's limiting beliefs?
2. What is an alternative belief that might be more freeing and give Jack a broader perspective?

3. How does Jack's current perspective restrict his company's growth?

4. If you were an associate of Jack's, how might you use a different perspective to help influence Jack's perspective?

5. How could Jack change his perspective?

REFERENCES

1. Levering, R., *A Great Place to Work,* New York: Random House, 1988.

2. Losoncy, L., *The Motivating Leader,* New York: Simon & Schuster, 1992.

3. Simon, S., *Getting Unstuck,* New York: Warner Books, 1988.

4. Cox, A., *Straight Talk for Monday Morning,* New York: John Wiley & Sons, 1990.

5. Levine, S. and Crom, M., *The Leader in You,* New York: Simon & Schuster, 1993, p. 87.

6. Levine, S. and Crom, M., *The Leader in You,* New York: Simon & Schuster, 1993.

7. Plunkett, L. and Fournier, R., *Participative Management: Implementing Empowerment,* New York: John Wiley & Sons, 1991.

6

ENCOURAGEMENT TRAINING

"Caste and class are real issues in organizations, as they are in the rest of society. But in the confined spaces of a plant or corporate headquarters, it is amazing that so much social distance can exist."

Woodrow Sears, Jr.

INTRODUCTION

How employees view their leader affects their attitude toward their work. Every decision, policy, and change that the leader makes teaches the entire work group what the leader believes. Employees closely observe the leader's behavior and learn to trust it more than his or her words. A leader's behavior either encourages or discourages employees. The impact is contagious; it affects each worker's attitude and performance.

Modeling encouragement is the most powerful way to teach encouragement. According to Allan Cox, "An executive indicates he or she possesses high self-esteem when he or she encourages an associate."[1]

"The man who believes he can do something is probably right, and so is the man who believes he can't."

Anonymous

THE PSYCHOLOGICAL BASIS OF ENCOURAGEMENT TRAINING

Effective leadership is based on a psychologically sound theory of human behavior that enables the leader to encourage the best from employees. Motivation in business and industry is often based on punishment and reward. Those who cooperate are rewarded; those who do not are punished. In this type of atmosphere, many employees feel that they are not treated with respect and resist cooperating. Encouragement is a system that focuses on the agreements and similarities between employer and employees. Encouragement fuels a person's resources and strengths in order to build self-esteem. As self-esteem increases, employees develop a desire to cooperate for the common good.

All human behavior is goal directed and has a purpose. Motivation is most effective when we understand each person's goals and work to align the goals of the organization and the leader with those of the individual. In planning to motivate someone, it is essential to be in touch with his or her goals. Behavior always makes sense when we understand goals.

For example, Andy has always given his secretaries orders. However, when he hired Sue, she resisted being told what to do. Andy had to learn what motivated Sue. As the oldest child in her family, she was accustomed to giving the orders and being independent. Now she was expected to take orders and be dependent. The result was a power struggle whenever Andy gave Sue an assignment. As Andy talked with Sue about her goals, they developed a cooperative relationship. He learned to give her control of certain areas, which satisfied her need to be in charge and, at the same time, reduced his workload. The stress was minimized and productivity increased.

All human behavior is social and is influenced by relationships with others. A manager who wants to motivate employees needs to understand the social meaning of their behavior. For example, what is the meaning of rebellious behavior or apathy? Some of the resistance may stem from a need for recognition or status.

We all have a basic need or desire to belong. Belonging is an important element in an individual's search for significance. A person is more fulfilled or self-actualized when he or she feels accepted as an integral part of a group.

It is important for an organization to provide both financial rewards and recognition. Leaders need to understand how each person wants to be recognized and accepted. When employees are recognized for being a part of a work team, they are likely to work more harmoniously toward the goals of the team and the organization. If they only get attention by being rebellious and cantankerous, then they will play to the audience that listens to and supports them.

Encouragement is always individualized by understanding how an individual perceives the world. Behavior is always influenced by a person's perception and interpretation of an event. An individual's perception is the basis of his or her interactions with others.

THE GOALS OF ENCOURAGEMENT TRAINING

The goals of encouragement training are the development of:

1. Positive self-esteem, positive self-awareness, positive self-image, and a belief in self

2. A self-motivated person who knows what needs to be done and accomplishes it

3. Positive self-expectations, whereby a person expects to succeed and looks for alternatives when he or she does not

4. A goal-oriented individual who understands the goals of the organization, its leaders, and its employees and can harmoniously align these goals

5. The ability to identify and own one's own strengths and utilize them for the common good and for personal and organizational growth

6. An empathic person who listens to feelings and intentions as well as content and can respond so that the other person feels understood (see Appendix #10, Encouragement Training)

SELF-ESTEEM VERSUS EGO ESTEEM

If people are to put all their efforts and resources into a task, they need positive self-esteem. Self-esteem produces positive beliefs and behavior. Ego esteem, on the other hand, involves competing, comparing, and feeling inadequate. Ego esteem is sometimes confused with self-esteem, but the two are quite different.

Self-esteem	*Ego esteem*
Is courageous, can take a risk	Motivated by fear of not being outstanding
Motivated by internal controls; feels good about self and is concerned about what others think	Motivated by external controls ("I am the important one")
Feels respected ("I'm okay")	Feel unappreciated ("Nobody cares")
Has a strong sense of purpose	Finds little meaning or purpose in tasks; just goes through the motions
Is creative and spontaneous	Is rigid and compulsive
Recognizes that no one is to blame but all are responsible for resolving roadblocks and problems	Blames others

People with self-esteem possess self-worth, self-respect, and self-confidence. They can view failure, lack of progress, and mistakes as corrective feedback instead of devastating experiences. They value and respect themselves. These traits enable them to put their full energy into their work because they are not distracted by secondary issues.

Self-determining people are aware that they have choices; they take responsibility by making their own decisions. They push their own buttons. Life is not an accident and they are not victims.

Goal-oriented people find life full of meaning and purpose. They set goals and move toward them deliberately. Self-motivated people move in the direction of the goals they establish. They intend to succeed. While they may encounter occasional roadblocks and obstacles, they see nothing that permanently separates them from their goals. Confronted with a problem, they focus on solutions and see the positive potential in any situation.

Positive self-image results when behavior is consistent with beliefs; it becomes a self-fulfilling prophecy.

> "No one can persuade another to change. Each of us guards a gate of change that can only be opened from the inside. We cannot open the gate of another, either by argument or emotional appeal."
>
> Marilyn Ferguson

ORGANIZATIONS THAT ENCOURAGE

Organizations that function in an encouraging manner do not happen by chance. They are the result of leaders who understand human behavior and motivation. These leaders intentionally encourage and build employee self-esteem at all levels.

In order for an organization to be encouraging, it is essential that the goals of the organization and the goals of individuals are aligned. Everyone must participate in planning, decision making, and the way the organization functions.

There are many opportunities for training in the encouragement process when:

1. The method of evaluation and appraisal employed by the organization is based on encouragement

2. There is daily recognition and appreciation of each leader for demonstrating encouraging behavior in contacts with colleagues, subordinates, and superiors

3. Encouragement and focusing on the positive and possibilities become the norm in leader–employee relationships

4. Finding fault and blaming are avoided

5. The emphasis in performance reviews is on improvement in future work or behavior instead of primarily criticism of what happened in the past

With training, leaders can become consistent and effective encouragers by:

1. Developing a positive focus on each person's behavior and commenting on anything potentially positive

2. Affirming any positive thoughts, actions, or intentions

3. Keeping a daily log of the encouragement they give

When an organization is encouraging, productivity and involvement are enhanced. The members of the organization derive some of their self-esteem and feelings of worth from involvement in the organization. They are proud of the organization and of being a significant part of it.

"**L**eaders need to foster environments and work processes within which people can develop high quality relationships—relationships

with each other, relationships with the group with which we work,
relationships with our clients and customers."

Max Depree

An encouraging organization also stimulates a belief in the value of its
objectives. People want to be a part of the group effort, to belong, to
cooperate, and to develop individual goals that are aligned with those of
the organization. Individual productivity is usually increased as organizational goals and personal goals are aligned. Employees work toward the
goals of the organization because it is mutually beneficial to do so.

For example, Mary is presently a secretary but she is ambitious and
wants to become a marketing executive. Frank, her manager, recognizes
her ambition. Whenever possible, he encourages her to get some experience working in marketing. He recognizes that when she feels satisfied
and recognized, she is more productive.

DEVELOPING THE FOUNDATION FOR ENCOURAGEMENT SKILLS

The goals of the organization and the goals of the leader need to be
shared openly and congruently in order to provide an atmosphere that is
encouraging. Internal control, a strong sense of purpose, interdependence,
creativity, and courage are developed as employee self-esteem increases.
The leader's goal is to increase the self-esteem of each employee, thereby
reducing competitiveness and resistance. This also results in increased
cooperation, involvement, commitment, responsibility, and productivity.

Responsibility is best developed by preparing the employees to accept
responsibility and then giving it to them. As employees begin to assume
their new responsibilities, the leader needs to focus on any positive
movement, effort, or contribution and recognize each individual's resources and potential. The leader should expect people to be responsible.
As people feel trusted and accepted, they are comfortable taking on added
responsibilities.

Communicating respect for individuals starts at the top. As top executives give credit where it is due, through memos, telephone calls, and
personal contacts, respect usually becomes mutual.

Most American organizations are jungles of competition among executives, managers, and employees. This waste of energy is created by a
management philosophy based on competition and a win–lose mentality.
Cooperation is built as individuals avoid competition with each other and
build mutual respect.

An encouraging organization recognizes the uniqueness of each individual and values differences. The leaders develop an organization that recognizes and rewards both cooperation and productivity.

ENCOURAGEMENT TRAINING: A COMPETENCY-BASED PROGRAM

Encouragement training is a skill development program. The skills required to be encouraging include attending, listening, responding, empathizing, identifying similarities, seeing perceptual alternatives, and developing responsibility in others (see Appendix #3, The Special Language of Encouragement).

Attending

The basic skill for improving communication in order to encourage is attending. The person who is attending conveys full attention. He or she is physically relaxed, leans forward, and makes eye contact. This indicates that he or she is ready to give full attention and energy to the other person and closely follow what is being discussed.

Attending also involves helping the other person feel comfortable. It conveys a receptive presence. There is complete involvement with the other person. Replies note the other person's concerns. The encourager does not respond to the other person's statements by discussing his or her own concerns or changing the subject.

Attending includes body language that communicates involvement and interest. Yawning, raising eyebrows, folding arms, watching the clock, answering the telephone, or appearing preoccupied and disinterested all communicate nonlistening and indifference.

Attending means awareness of the other person's body language. It is estimated that over 80 percent of our communication is nonverbal. Attending to how a person sits, stands, and gestures helps the encourager to hear unspoken words.

Suppose Bill has just finished an important telephone call and is reorganizing his schedule as a result of the call. Joe knocks at his door and says, "I need to see you." Bill's typical response used to be to defer the contact. Instead, he gets up from his chair, welcomes Joe, and says, "I only have five or ten minutes, but tell me your concern." He leans forward, establishes eye contact, and attends to Joe's verbal and nonverbal behavior.

Listening

The first step in listening is to actively and deliberately communicate the intent to listen and understand. The encouraging leader stays with the issue that is presented. There are no interruptions, distractions, or attempts to change the subject. All distractions that indicate nonlistening, such as looking away or glancing at papers, are avoided.

> "**O**f all the skills of leadership, listening is one of the most valuable—and one of the least understood. Most captains of industry listen only sometimes, and they remain ordinary leaders. But a few, the great ones, never stop listening. They are hear-aholics, ever alert, bending their ears while they work and while they play, while they eat and while they sleep. They listen to advisers, to customers, to inner voices, to enemies, to the wind. That's how they get word before anyone else of unseen problems and opportunities."
>
> *Fortune*

Listening involves taking the time to get to know someone better and giving him or her the feeling of being valued and appreciated. A major complaint of employees is that they do not feel appreciated. Listening communicates that the other person can feel safe, is not intruding on your time, and has valuable ideas.

In the following scenario, Leo comes in to see his manager, Marge, about a problem he is having:

> *Leo:* "I'm having a hard time meeting the schedule, and the new men you have working with me are inexperienced."
>
> *Marge* (nonlistening): "Well, that's why I put them with you, to get training. With three of you, you should be able to finish everything."
>
> *Marge* (listening): "You're discouraged about the schedule and feel the men are slowing you down."

Exercise

Respond with listening to the following:

> When can we expect to get organized so the schedule doesn't change each week? I'm tired of the confusion.

Your response:

"**W**hen I listened most closely I could hear the unheard...To hear the unheard is a necessary discipline to be a good ruler. For only when a ruler has learned to listen closely to the people's hearts, hearing their feelings uncommunicated, pains unexpressed, and complaints not spoken of, can he hope to inspire confidence in his people, understand when something is wrong, and meet the true needs of his citizens. The demise of states comes when leaders listen only to superficial words and do not penetrate deeply into the soul of the people to hear their true opinions, feelings, and desires."

C.W. Kim and Renee A. Mauborgne
Harvard Business Review

Responding

Encouragers respond by using active listening; that is, they put the speaker's thoughts into their own words. They listen to the whole message and indicate that they understand the meaning. The encouraging person is open to whatever is expressed.

A closed response is like a question in that it asks for specific information and expects a specific response ("When did this arrive?" "What is the price?" "What will you do?"). An open response accurately restates what has been said ("You are concerned about this being late." "You are worried that this will exceed the budget." "I hear you say that you are having a problem with this process."). This allows the speaker to further express his or her feelings, beliefs, attitudes, and values. Being understood conveys a feeling of acceptance.

The listener's response often affects what the speaker will say next. If you respond only to beliefs, then the other person will discuss beliefs. If you respond to feelings, the other person is likely to discuss feelings.

As the conversation progresses, an open response allows the speaker to steer the conversation in the most productive direction. As you hear beliefs, feelings, perceptions, and goals, you can choose those to which you will respond. If you select the feelings of greatest meaning to the other person, the result will be satisfying communication.

> "The missing link between corporations and the customer
> is the human touch."
>
> C. Westland

Personal responses improve as one learns to listen for the themes and feelings behind the words and for the nonverbal messages. The result is often a mutually satisfying two-way dialogue.

In responding, it is important to avoid the following response styles that discourage:

1. *The commander-in-chief*—Controls, orders, and commands

2. *The moralist*—Focuses on "shoulds" and preaches

3. *The judge*—Is judgmental and concerned with being right

4. *The critic*—Uses ridicule and sarcasm in overcoming the other person and proving himself or herself right

5. *The consoler*—Is not really involved; simply reassures

6. *The avoider*—Fails to respond to real issues

When you respond encouragingly, you:

1. Become a mirror that reflects back to the other person what he or she is experiencing

2. Avoid interrupting

3. Stay on the topic presented

4. Permit silences, as they stimulate growth; by attending closely and being silent, you demonstrate that what the other person is saying is vital

5. Focus on what the message means to the speaker instead of how it affects you

6. Avoid becoming involved in trying to win, one-upmanship, or arguing

7. Listen to the whole message instead of interrupting

8. Verbalize the key issue as the speaker sees it

Exercise

In three communication situations you have in the next two days, be aware of how your responding affects the process and the relationship.

Considerations in Workplace Communication

A Linguistic Model of Workplace Communication

Fernando Flores[2,3] adapted the work of British linguists Austin and Searle to espouse the following four basic communication activities or "speech acts" that people use in order to get positive results.

1. We *ask* others to do things:

    "Please have this report on my desk by noon."

    "Please help us out on this project."

2. We *promise* others that we will do things or we refuse (promise *not*) to do them:

    "I'll meet you Friday morning at eleven."

    "I am not willing to work overtime again this weekend."

    At other times, requests and promises are combined or negotiated in such conditional offers as:

    "Give me two days and I'll have the proposal on your desk."

    "If you can't improve your price, we'll have to take our business elsewhere."

3. We *assert* that certain things are either true or false:

    "There are five critical factors in making our decision."

    "The rumor of your demotion is totally untrue."

4. Leaders use their authenticity to *declare* things to be valid or invalid for themselves and others:

    "I will become a project supervisor."

    "That project is not a priority for us right now."

Four key communication questions arise from such a basic "asking," "promising," "asserting," and "declaring" model:

1. Did one of us ask or demand something of the other?

2. Did one of us promise (or refuse) something to the other?

3. What did either of us assert to be true or false?

4. Did either of us declare or define something (i.e., did we commit ourselves to a new direction, definition, attitude, or state of affairs regarding our work together)?

Multicultural Communication Considerations

Communication with someone of another culture requires a special commitment to take extra time to focus on the interpretation. Here are ten basic recommendations for maximizing culturally diverse understanding:

1. ***Slow down; speak slowly and distinctly.***

2. ***Use basic vocabulary and keep it simple.*** Say "I want to talk with you this morning" instead of "I need to have a conversation with you at your earliest possible convenience."

3. ***Listen actively.*** Periodically check to see if you are being accurately heard and also paraphrase what you are hearing.

4. ***Repeat, rephrase, and illustrate messages.*** Give your message in several different ways when speaking English to someone whose native language is not English.

5. ***Avoid slang, jargon, and colloquial expressions.*** The response to "Where are you coming from?" may be a person's home town or last destination. A postal clerk once asked a recent immigrant, "How's it going?" and got the reply, "Airmail."

6. ***Use acronyms sparingly.*** The military is especially fond of acronyms, and they often bear little resemblance to the words being abbreviated. For example, ESL stands for the social action unit in the Air Force. While NATO, IRS, GMAC, OPEC, and NAFTA are convenient ways to shorten phrases, many people are unaware of the meaning of such abbreviations.

7. ***Rehearse your humor.*** Humor frequently relies on intricate language nuances and too often belittles racial or ethnic groups. Whenever possible, rehearse a joke with someone who knows or is from the culture to be addressed before using a joke in public.

8. ***Expect delayed reactions.*** It simply takes longer to translate and encode from one language to another.

9. ***Don't assume congruence.*** Remember that your private logic, or cultural experience, is unique to you. It will not necessarily be understood by someone from another culture. This is especially true of metaphors. For example, Simons, Vazquez, and Harris quote a Japanese negotiator who observed that "American business people are like hunters. They go on expeditions and expect to fire a couple of shots and come home with a trophy. My

people, on the other hand, do business like we farm. We carefully plant and water and hope for many harvests from the same field."

10. ***Use visual aids and/or handouts.*** Recognize that it is frustrating for people whose native language is not English to try to simultaneously translate and take notes during a presentation delivered by an English-speaking businessperson who is reading from a set of neatly typed notes. Provide handouts whenever possible and use simple pictures and diagrams to illustrate key concepts.[4]

Valuing diversity in the workplace is a frequent theme in many business workshops and seminars. Five specific ways of valuing diversity are suggested in *Leadership and the Customer Revolution:*

1. ***Reward people who continually question present practices.*** Most organizations need more questioning, more experimentation, and more innovative attempts to redefine the way work is done.

2. ***Promote weirdness.*** Until being different is perceived to be career-enhancing, organizations will never capture the full benefits of a diverse work force.

3. ***Analyze the business from a competitor's point of view.*** Challenge a group to devise a plan to put their own organization "out of business" by coming up with a unique way to add substantially more value for customers.

4. ***Reward experimentation: love the .500 hitter.*** Without the ability to fail, there is less questioning, less experimentation, less learning, and, therefore, no transformational improvement.

5. ***Redouble education efforts! Ensure inconsistencies!*** It is helpful to select educators who hold very different views from those in the organization and who offer a different perspective from other educators.[5]

Empathizing

Empathy is responding to the feeling being expressed rather than responding solely to the content. It indicates to the speaker that the listener hears his or her feelings and beliefs, recognizes them, and is willing to accept them. What the speaker said is fully heard, understood, and reflected.

An empathic response expresses the other person's feelings and meanings in ways that facilitate his or her self-expression and self-understanding. It does not go past the feeling, but deals with it. Examples of empathic responses include: "You're angry and upset." "That seems unfair." "You're proud of your work team's efforts this month." "You're suspicious that accounting is hiding the facts."

After experiencing empathy, a person is more likely to express additional feelings and concerns. Empathy supplies motivation for the ongoing communication process between two people or between a leader and a group.

Exercise

Respond empathically to the following communications:

> "I'm tired of having to take on extra work because other people don't do their jobs."

Your response:

> "I've been here two years, and you've never given me any recognition or respect."

Your response:

Leaders need to understand what their employees value. Alfred Adler believed that understanding another person's basic lifestyle is the highest form of empathy in action. A familiar American Indian saying is, "If you want to know my world, then walk a mile in my moccasins."

Words that encourage take into account a person's need for both relationship and meaning. An empathic response communicates an understanding and an appreciation of the other person's private world. Just feeling heard and understood by someone else is often all that someone needs.

> "Always treat your employees
> exactly as you want them to treat your best customers."
>
> Stephen R. Covey

Identifying Similarities

Identifying common goals, interests, and themes can help bridge the gap between a leader and an employee and create a feeling of equality. Identifying similarities means finding common feelings, beliefs, perceptions, and attitudes.

Exercise

Make a list of the people on your staff. Note similarities between you and each of them (e.g., "We both care about people" or "We both give full effort").

Seeing Perceptual Alternatives

The encouraging leader can see the positive potential in any person or situation. For example, when confronted with a slow market, the encouraging leader tests new marketing and advertising strategies and conducts intensive in-house training. In dealing with a resistant employee, the encouraging leader looks for positive traits; perhaps, for example, the stubborn employee is also very determined. Instead of criticizing the employee for resisting supervision, the encouraging leader focuses on the employee's determination to see how his or her goals can be matched with those of the job and the organization.

A problem is a challenge and an opportunity to extend creative thinking. Perceptual alternatives are different ways of viewing and giving meaning to a situation. Using perceptual alternatives involves being creative. For example, if a purchasing agent finds that he bought too much material at too high a price, the encouraging manager could respond by saying, "Can anything be done about this purchase now?" or "What did we learn from this?" or "How do you plan to deal with this supplier next time?"

These are alternative, constructive approaches to errors that people make. How a manager handles such situations either tears an employee down or builds his or her self-esteem to do better next time. Seeing a problem as a challenge and an opportunity can motivate employees and increase productivity.

Developing Responsibility and Productivity in Others

To develop responsibility and productivity in employees, recognize their resources, assets, and potentials. Give employees assignments in which they can succeed and develop confidence. As you learn to identify what you have in common with the people with whom you are speaking, you begin to feel closer to them. You are not comfortable labeling their differences. Instead, you are in a relationship that communicates understanding, belonging, and acceptance. Your goal is to help them feel that they are contributing while allowing them to grow, by using their assets and tapping their potential.

Encouraging leaders focus on efforts and contributions. They recognize energy and enthusiasm. The employee who gives 100 percent and really tries, even though not totally productive, feels appreciated when he or she hears, "You gave it your best shot, and I appreciate that."

Responsibility does not result from constant checking and "snoopervision." It comes from faith and positive expectations. When responsible behavior is expected, it is achieved.

Exercise

Think of your best boss or mentor as you were developing your leadership skills. List the things your boss or mentor did to develop your responsibility and productivity.

What do you regularly do to develop your associates' responsibility and productivity?

LEADERSHIP BY ENCOURAGEMENT AND FROM THE HEART

In *Managing from the Heart,* Bracey et al. use the acronym HEART to highlight the leadership skills being requested by contemporary workers:

> *Hear and understand me.* When one listens actively, a primary focus is on content, information, and ideas. But attitudes, intentions, and feelings are also important parts of active listening.

> *Even if you disagree, please don't make me wrong.* You can still have reactions, but let your words be about you and how you view the situation. Start your sentences with the word "I" and finish them by describing your state of mind, your feelings, or your wishes. The other person can then take your statements or leave them.

> *Acknowledge the greatness within me.* Everyone has potential for growth, respect, appreciation, and encouragement. People tend to respond positively to anyone who identifies their potential greatness, especially if no such evidence has surfaced.

> *Remember to look for my loving intentions.* This involves going beyond merely hearing the other person. It involves appreciating the intention behind what the person says. Not looking for a loving intention is a subtle way of looking for devious motives. This does not imply that you will actually find loving intentions everywhere. Rather, it is a commitment to look for them.

> *Tell me the truth with compassion.* Constructive confrontation does not mean avoiding confronting a worker when necessary; rather, it suggests adding the skills of firmness and caring. The first step in effective confrontation is speaking directly to the person involved instead of talking to someone else. Do not confront an employee in front of others. Listen to his or her side of the story, and then observe that the specific behavior is actually changed.

Leadership by encouragement is symbolized by the universal sign of caring and compassion: the heart. Too often, management is from the head with logic and from the spleen or solar plexus with anger. Leaders can use statistical analyses, market forecasts, and economic indicators, which Bracey et al. define as "head tools." Power, bullying, ridicule, and sarcasm are "spleen tools." An approach from the heart is crucial to being an effective encouraging leader.[6]

The Wal-Mart Story

The founding of Wal-Mart is an example of leadership by encouragement. Wal-Mart was founded in 1962 by Sam Walton, the owner of several Ben Franklin stores. Because of its extraordinary growth at a compound rate of 25 percent per year from 1960 to 1990, and because it reaped an average annual return of 45 percent for its investors from 1977 to 1987, in 1989 Wal-Mart was named Retailer of the Decade by *Discount Store News*. In 1992, Walton was named to the National Business Hall of Fame.

One of the keys to Wal-Mart's success is that, from the outset, Walton recognized the importance of employees, whom he called associates. Walton followed three fundamental principles in working with his associates:

1. Treat employees as partners. Share with them both the good news and the bad so they will strive to excel. Allow them to share in the rewards of their achievements.

2. Encourage employees to always challenge the obvious. The road to success includes failing, which is part of the learning process rather than a personal or corporate defect or shortcoming.

3. Involve associates at all levels in the total decision-making process.

As one busy holiday season approached, Walton appeared on a satellite broadcast to all his Wal-Mart associates. Wearing his trademark baseball cap, he made the following modest proposal to them: "Whenever customers approach, look them in the eye, greet them, and ask to help." Realizing that some associates were shy, Walton encouraged them by saying, "It would, I'm sure, help you become a leader. It would help your personality develop; you would become more outgoing; and in time you might become manager of the store...or whatever you choose to be in the company....It will do wonders for you."

Walton then had his associates raise their right hands and execute a pledge to remind them that "a promise we make is a promise we keep." The pledge was: "From this day forward, I solemnly promise and declare that every customer who comes within ten feet of me, I will smile, look them in the eye, and greet them, so help me Sam."

Psychiatrist Rudolf Dreikurs is noted for the following admonition: "Have the courage to be imperfect." An example of making the most of a mistake occurred at Wal-Mart in 1985, when John Lave, assistant store manager in Oneonta, Alabama, accidentally ordered four times the usual number of Moon Pies (a marshmallow cookie made by Chattanooga Bakeries). Although most companies would have fired him for such a major mistake, his boss simply encouraged him to use his imagination in finding a way to sell them. The result was a Moon Pie-eating contest held in the Wal-Mart parking lot. The event was so successful that it is now held annually.[7]

> "**M**anagement means, in the last analysis, the substitution of thought for brawn and muscle, of knowledge for folkways and superstition, and of cooperation for force. It means the substitution of responsibility for obedience to rank, and of authority of performance for the authority of rank."
>
> Peter Drucker

The Semco Story

Richard Semler has written an inspiring book entitled *Maverick* in which he describes both the radical and widely successful story of Semco, a Brazilian company he inherited from his father. Semler's management system allows employees to work at home, study and discuss the company's financial statements, make corporate decisions, take over the cafeteria kitchen, start their own business with company assets, and redesign Semco products. The staggering result of this unorthodox approach is that over the past ten years, as Brazil's overall economy declined, Semco has achieved a growth rate of 600 percent!

Semco has been visited by over 400 international corporate representatives. The company's last job posting generated 1400 responses, in addition to 2000 existing unsolicited resumes. A recent poll indicated that 20 percent of all college students in Brazil said they would like to work for Semco when they graduate. In 1993, CEO Ricardo Semler was voted Business Leader of the Year by 52,000 conservative business leaders and hailed by the Marxist union leaders as "the only trustworthy boss in the country."

While his approach will surely be viewed as radical by most business leaders, his huge success is directly correlated to his philosophy of encouraging his employees. Semler[8] observes that

"Almost all businessmen think their employees are involved in the firm and are its greatest asset.

Almost all employees think they are given too little attention and respect, and cannot say what they really think.

The sad truth is employees of modern corporations have little reason to feel satisfied, much less fulfilled. Companies do not have the time or the interest to listen to them, and lack the resources or the inclination to train them for advancement. These companies make a series of demands, for which they compensate employees with salaries that are often considered inadequate. Moreover, companies tend to be implacable in dismissing workers when they start to age or go through a temporary drop in performance, and send people into retirement earlier than they want, leaving them with the feeling they could have contributed much more had someone just asked.

The era of using people as production tools is coming to an end. Participation is infinitely more complex to practice than conventional corporate unilateralism, just as democracy is much more cumbersome than dictatorship. But there will be few companies that can afford to ignore either of them."

Semler also uses a creative metaphor by observing that the pyramid, the chief organizational principle of the modern corporation, turns a business into a "traffic jam." A company starts out like an eight-lane superhighway (the bottom of the pyramid), drops six lanes, then four, then two, then becomes a country road, and eventually a dirt path, before abruptly coming to a stop. Thousands of drivers start off on the highway, but as it narrows, more and more are forced to slow and stop. There are smash-ups and cars are pushed off onto the shoulder. Some drivers give up and take side roads to other destinations. A few—the most aggressive—keep charging ahead, swerving and accelerating and bending fenders all about them. Remember, objects in the mirror are closer than they appear.[8]

KEY POINTS

1. The single most important factor in being a successful leader is the perception that every employee has of the leader.

2. Policies, procedures, and attitudes comprise leadership style.

3. Employees learn to trust actions more than words.

4. In planning to motivate a person, it is essential to know his or her goals.

5. An organization should help its members fulfill their individual search for significance.

6. Low self-esteem can involve people in competing, comparing, and feeling inadequate.

7. An important goal is developing self-motivated employees.

8. A successful organization encourages alignment of its goals with those of individual members.

9. Encouragement skills include attending, listening, responding, empathizing, identifying similarities, seeing perceptual alternatives, and developing responsibility and productivity in others.

LEADERSHIP BY ENCOURAGEMENT APPLICATIONS

Encouragement training in an organization is daily and continuous through the modeling of encouraging leadership. Systematic training sessions are also necessary.

1. How do your associates perceive you? How do your policies and decisions teach them your beliefs?

2. How does your organization clearly communicate the encouragement process?

3. How would you establish an encouragement training program in your organization?

ENCOURAGEMENT SKILLS

1. Do a self-inventory and identify all of your strengths and resources. Remember, your resources are not derived from comparison with others; they what you feel good about in yourself.

2. Eliminate from your thinking any fear of failure, because it keeps you from valuing yourself. Instead, look for possibilities and opportunities. Be in touch with your self-confidence.

3. Know your uniqueness and potential, and use your resources with your associates.

4. Own your strengths. Give yourself affirmations and positive messages, such as "I am capable" or "People like me."

5. Be intrinsically motivated and focus on your efforts and assets. Increase the joy in your life by being enthusiastic without comparisons.

Vignette

Shirley is the leader of a marketing team. The team has several projects that were minimally successful. Shirley recognizes that Jack, Betty, and Sam are all very discouraged and lack confidence in their ability to develop successful campaigns. Shirley is even beginning to question her own ability to supply encouraging and motivating leadership to the team.

1. How you would begin to change the situation?

2. What are some personal affirmations you could use as the leader?

3. How would you help the members of the team to become more self-encouraged?

REFERENCES

1. Cox, A., *The Making of the Achiever,* New York: Dodd, Mead, 1985.

2. Flores, F., *Management & Communication in the Office of the Future*, unpublished monograph, 1982.

3. Flores, F. and Wenograd, L., *Understanding Cognition*, Reading, MA: Addison Wesley, 1987.

4. Simons, G., Vazquez, C., and Harris, P., *Transcultural Leadership: Empowering the Diverse Workforce*, Houston: Gulf Publishing, 1993.

5. Heil, G., Parkes, T., and Tate, R., *Leadership and the Customer Revolution*, New York: Van Nostrand Reinhold, 1995.

6. Bracey, H., Rosenblum, J., Sanford, A., and Trueblood, R., *Managing from the Heart,* New York: Delacorte Press, 1990.

7. Boyett, J. and Conn, H., *Workplace 2000: The Revolution Reshaping American Business,* New York: Dutton, 1991.

8. Semler, R., *Maverick*, New York: Warner, 1993, p. 106.

7

PARTICIPATIVE MANAGEMENT AS ENCOURAGEMENT

INTRODUCTION

Participative management is a logical extension of the psychology of encouragement. As leaders and associates develop mutual respect, involvement, and commitment to their common goals, the stage is set for the development of participative management. Participative management is a leadership philosophy underlying a wide range of employee involvement efforts. It is based on the concept that employees closest to the job have the necessary experience and knowledge to develop the best solutions to job-related problems. Participative management can help tap unused human resources by increasing employee involvement on the job and commitment to organizational goals, as well as improving the quality of work.

Participative management creates an opportunity to provide encouragement, share authority, and empower people. As workers are included and shown respect, they become more involved in developing solutions and being responsible for their own behavior. Solutions are reached in a more systematic and effective manner. This often results in increased productivity for the leader, as he or she is free to do more planning and higher level tasks.

181

Through the work of Peters and Waterman,[1-3] there has been an increased emphasis on the importance of developing excellence in corporations. Excellence results from having clear goals and from involving employees appropriately in decision making. As workers participate in making decisions and contribute productively to the organization, their feelings of belonging, pride in ownership, and responsibility result in benefits to the organization as well as to themselves. Each person becomes fully responsible for his or her actions and results. Blaming is minimized, and problem solving and learning take its place. This is the atmosphere in which a "learning organization" can be created.

When an organization decides to switch to participative management and leadership by encouragement, it recognizes that people are motivated by their own goals and by a feeling of belonging. As individual goals and organizational goals are aligned, unproductive tension is reduced and productive energy is created from working together instead of in competition.

In describing the "six R's of motivation," Marsh (p. 26) says: "The three traditional motivation techniques—the threat, the carrot (bribery), and the instructions—need to be abandoned. Motivation is achieved by an attitude that will produce enthusiasm and commitment." The following six R's of motivation are very powerful in achieving this attitude:

1. Review and plan with the staff to secure their involvement.

2. Responsibility must be shared by all, not just the manager.

3. Reward adequately and creatively to show appreciation.

4. Recognize achievements.

5. Respect staff as individuals who have commitments outside the workplace.

6. Report progress to the employees, praising successes and highlighting areas where improvements can be made.[4]

TEAM means *T*ogether *E*veryone *A*chieves *M*ore.

THE PSYCHOLOGY OF PARTICIPATIVE MANAGEMENT

The psychology of participative management assumes that individuals choose, decide, and act in terms of their goals and purposes. Goals are the final explanation for all behavior. All motivation is based on understanding goals. Leaders work to help individuals accomplish individual goals that fit with organizational goals. Goal setting that includes the individual's needs as well as those of the organization energizes the work process.

Discouraged employees lack self-esteem and a desire to cooperate; they often believe that they cannot be successful in an active, constructive way, so they tend to be passive and resist cooperating to the fullest. They may be late, absent, uncooperative, or passive rebels.

Participative managers need to identify the positive potential in every situation and in every person. This requires the ability to develop perceptual alternatives—to see the strengths, not the weaknesses, and to see possibilities, not just limitations. The employee who is resistant also has the potential to use his or her determination for a positive purpose.

Participative management leaders are not concerned with having power over their employees. Their goal is to empower their employees to feel more capable, more independent, more involved, and more responsible.

> "There is only one way under high heaven to get anyone to do anything. Did you ever think about it? Yes, just one way. And that is by making the other person want to do it."
>
> Dale Carnegie

CHARACTERISTICS OF PARTICIPATIVE MANAGEMENT

1. Participative management develops ownership thinking at all levels of the organization. All employees become protective of company resources and enthusiastic about organizational progress. There is a feeling of emotional and financial investment in the organization.

2. An attitude of trust and respect prevails at all levels. Top management respects each employee and is, in turn, respected by all employees. A feeling of cooperation and unity is created.

3. Employees' goals are discovered and, through a mutual process, are aligned with the goals of the organization.

4. All employees take full responsibility for their actions and the results of their actions, both positive and negative. They may benefit as their contributions are recognized; however, they also accept responsibility for problems. The work atmosphere is characterized by courage; people believe in themselves, are confident, and are willing to take risks.

5. Ideas are expressed openly, with mutual participation in decision making. Top management actively seeks feedback, creating a feeling of full involvement in the organization. Suggestions are welcomed and acknowledged, and resulting actions are communicated throughout the organization.

6. Feedback is openly given and shared within the organization. It may be spontaneous, but it is also planned and scheduled through performance reviews, meetings, and other procedures. Feedback is both challenging and encouraging.

7. Leaders do not feel threatened by staff participation and involvement. Leaders' decisions are open to scrutiny. Employees have the right to ask questions and to express disagreement. Because there are channels for disagreement and dialogue, employees do not have to "go underground" and spread negative reactions. Managers are assessed, in part, on how much their employees feel understood.

8. Problems and changes are seen as opportunities to apply expertise and to develop options. A problem is a hurdle that can be overcome. Employees learn to regard change as a process that enables the organization to grow and develop.

PARTICIPATIVE PROBLEM SOLVING

When leadership by encouragement and participative management are established in an organization, the typical problems faced by leaders have a way of being resolved. The encouraging leader and participative management make employees responsible for solving problems, instead of just the managers. In an encouraging, participative atmosphere, problems are dealt with more effectively and efficiently.

When a performance problem is encountered, use of the improving management performance cycle (described in Chapter 4) is suggested. The improving management performance cycle is summarized as follows:

Step 1: Identify the issue. Get the clear facts and decide what the concern is. Often, the symptoms of the concern are not the real problem. Identify employee priorities, such as getting one's way, being in control, or being right.

The Kern Lifestyle Scale[5] is especially helpful in identifying the priorities of employees. It is efficient because it can be administered and scored in minutes. The Lifestyle Scale identifies such factors as:

1. Control

2. Perfectionism

3. Need to please

4. Victim

5. Martyr

Step 2: Inventory the assets. See the positive regardless of the situation. Employees should be encouraged to identify their own strengths and assets; the leader can then supplement such personal affirmations with his or her own observations.

Step 3: Goal setting and goal aligning. Establish clear performance standards which are achievable and realistic and which will secure the employee's involvement. The manager needs to identify how the goals of the employee can be aligned with those of the organization.

Step 4: Appraising performance. Once the goals are established and the projects begin, it is important to have a systematic and effective way to observe, evaluate, and give feedback on performance and progress.

Step 5: Consequences. Logical consequences are the result of the employee's performance. A variety of possible consequences exist. When an employee has functioned effectively, this is an opportunity to encourage or point out any progress that has been made.

An outstanding performance means the employee will be praised. However, when an employee makes a mistake or does not function effectively, it is important to advise him or her that you will be giving feedback privately. This will be the reprimand. Be specific about what you had anticipated happening and what is not happening. This type of feedback needs to be immediate. Keep your response brief and to the point and remember to criticize the behavior, not the person. This could be done with an "I" message such as "I feel very disappointed when you do not reach the quota because I thought we had planned a way this could happen" ("I feel…when…because…").

> "Teamwork is the essence of life."
>
> Pat Riley

THE USE OF SELF-DIRECTED WORK TEAMS

The use of self-directed work teams is an outstanding application of participative management. In a study conducted throughout the United States on the practices, roles, and results associated with the use of self-directed teams (SDTs), the following findings were reported:

1. Of the executives who responded to the survey, 26 percent indicated that they use SDTs in their organizations.

2. Many production tasks are handled by the team, while leadership tasks are still handled by a leader outside the team.

3. Team-based organizations offer training for job skills, team and interactive skills, and quality-action skills.

4. Executives listed insufficient training, supervisory resistance, and incompatible systems as the top three barriers to SDTs.

5. Respondents cited improved quality, improved productivity, heightened morale, and reduced labor costs as the most significant benefits of SDTs.[6]

> "**B**ecause consultants are outsiders and they
> don't know the corporate culture, they can ask
> the dumb questions that no one else would dare ask."
>
> Tom Ahern

A CASE STUDY OF LEADERSHIP BY ENCOURAGEMENT

The following is an illustration of how participative management and leadership by encouragement were established in one organization by Don Dinkmeyer. It demonstrates how certain basic steps facilitated movement toward participative management (see Appendix #2, The Encouragement Process).

The CEO–owner identified a need to increase leadership skills and responsibilities. At the same time, he identified a specific consultant who he believed would have a positive approach in dealing with the company's challenges.

The consultant and the CEO spent a great deal of time discussing the CEO's expectations, desires, and goals. The CEO clearly described the current status of the company, his objectives, and his ideas about how they might be achieved. The CEO wanted to develop a stable organization with a strong sales force.

Next, an executive evaluation and assessment was conducted with all potential leaders in the organization (see Appendix #13, Self-Evaluation and Assessment). The assessment focused on understanding the individuals' professional goals and expectations as well as the impact of lifestyle issues on the individuals. The respondents' family constellations (identification of siblings and birth order, i.e., oldest, middle, youngest, or only child) were assessed. Early recollections provided a window into how each person perceived life and life's tasks. The Kern Lifestyle Scale also was used. The assessment permitted the consultant to become better acquainted with each person and to obtain insight into his or her lifestyle, areas of satisfaction, resources, strengths, perception of present position, and things he or she would like to see changed.

The purpose of the assessment was to help potential leaders develop a better understanding of themselves and their strengths and resources. At the same time, the consultant became aware of individuals, relationships within the workplace, and people who could be used to increase cooperation and communication throughout the system.

The Interviewing Process

The consultant conducted individual interviews with each person assessed, beginning with the CEO. The CEO identified his leadership strengths as the ability to organize, to develop good game plans, to prioritize tasks, and to develop long-range strategies. His Kern Lifestyle Scale indicated a strong emphasis on his ability to lead and take charge. He saw himself as a problem solver. At the same time, he was a perfectionist; he set high standards for himself and for the people around him. This tended to frustrate workers who could not reach his standards. Furthermore, the CEO's self-esteem was relatively strong, and he was not particularly sensitive to others. At times, he took on more than he could do effectively, and he had a tendency to feel overwhelmed.

The CEO placed great emphasis on fairness in dealing with people, a strength in the development of participative management. He recognized the need for better knowledge of organization development, better communication skills, and better methods for developing leaders as facilitators.

The consultant then contacted three executive vice presidents with major leadership responsibilities in the organization. One was dissatisfied with his current position and wanted to be more involved with strategic planning, an area in which he thought the company was deficient.

The second vice president derived most satisfaction from nonwork aspects of her life. Her problems at work related to lack of resources and undefined roles and responsibilities of leaders.

The chief financial officer (CFO) appeared to be the most interested in contributing and working cooperatively. His challenges on the job resulted from competitiveness among the vice presidents and little appreciation by the staff directly under him. He also saw a need for more long-term planning (see Appendix #5, Evaluating Your Leadership Relations).

These three leaders did not provide a cooperative team approach. Two were more interested in personal advancement. The consultant developed a better knowledge of the leaders as well as the corporation through the individual interviews.

Additional interviews with other staff members revealed considerable dissatisfaction with two of the three leaders. Eventually, these two re-signed, reducing the leadership to the CEO and the CFO. This emphasized the need to develop leadership from within the company, a natural opportunity for a transition to participative management.

The CEO and the consultant met to clarify the type of leaders wanted. The CEO wanted leaders who:

1. Understood the resources available

2. Were sensitive to people and could inspire and motivate others to follow them

3. Knew the organizational structure

4. Were encouraging

5. Had the vision to see and evaluate opportunities to develop a profitable organization

Organizational Problems

There was no effective positive performance review system in the organization. Reviews were not systematic. They were not two-way reviews in which the leader also received feedback from employees. The consultant designed a performance review that would meet the company's needs and circulated it among the leaders and potential leaders.

There was a lack of individual goal setting and general management skills in the organization. The company reacted to the stresses and pressures that occurred daily and weekly rather than planning systematically to control its own destiny. The volume of work was uncontrollable at points, and no one seemed to take responsibility for controlling the work flow. Major problems included:

1. A lack of appreciation for the lower levels of staff who accomplished the major tasks that made the organization productive

2. Unclear responsibilities and leadership tasks

3. Poor communication within the organization

4. A widespread feeling of not belonging to a team

Communication and Training

The consultant was introduced to the entire staff, and his role was clarified. He was there to facilitate increased productivity and improve relations both within the company and in the marketplace. He expressed his belief that the people on staff were one of the company's major assets. An important focus was on developing the encouragement process—helping each employee feel valued, appreciated, involved, and responsible.

The consultant indicated that he would be getting to know individuals and their goals, objectives, and perceptions and that he and the employees, as a team, would develop a procedure to work systematically with both groups and individuals. After interviewing potential leaders in the organization, he began a series of classes focused on encouragement and communication.[7]

The atmosphere developed during the training was a model of what was anticipated in the total corporation. The focus was on improved communication and increased participation by all in decision making. Participation in profits was based on productivity and responsibility. The goal was to develop ownership and responsibility.

As full participation in the management of the company developed, it became apparent that a few of the participants interpreted it as an opportunity to criticize leadership. Some of the leaders saw it as more of a gripe session than a constructive building of relationships. This was confronted directly in ensuing seminars as an opportunity for everyone to become involved. The leaders also were concerned about people having the necessary information to support new responsibilities.

The CEO and the CFO agreed to clarify the organizational structure, job titles and responsibilities, and company goals and policies and to openly reveal financial information. This disclosure appeared to improve the level of employee trust. There was some concern that leadership by encouragement and participative management, as supported by the CEO and set forth by the consultant, might just be another fad. In an ensuing meeting, the CEO and the CFO discussed with the staff the fact that this was a permanent plan.

An experienced member of the organization was appointed head of marketing. The CFO remained in his position. A management team of five members was selected. It was their responsibility to join the CEO, the CFO, and the head of marketing in weekly meetings. It was also their responsibility to relay to the rest of the staff the information shared and decisions made at these meetings.

Classes for the management team were conducted on topics such as leadership, courage, decisiveness, assertiveness, encouragement, empowerment, vision, developing commitment, goal alignment, and positive performance appraisal. Encouragement groups for employees who were not on the management team also were established.

The major factors in helping this corporation become successful were:

- A growing attitude of trust and respect was developed at all levels.

- The goals of the leaders and the employees became increasingly congruent.

- All employees were paid according to their participation in the profits, which increased trust in the leaders' willingness to back up their philosophy with dollars.

As all employees participated in regular meetings with their leaders, the organizational goals became better understood and more accepted. Each employee began to take full responsibility for actions and ensuing results. Now the focus in the organization is on developing solutions rather than presenting problems or placing blame. A basic belief is that everyone is responsible and no one is to blame.

SUMMARY

Participative management is a human relations approach to leadership that is built upon a solid set of psychological concepts and methods. A managerial method for resolving conflict and moving toward cooperation and productivity is basic to implementing change. Human resource departments and business and organizational consultants trained in psychology put such programs into action.

KEY POINTS

1. Participative management is a logical extension of the psychology of encouragement.

2. People are the most underdeveloped resource of companies. They are "human capital."

3. Excellence results from each person being held fully responsible for his or her actions.

4. The goal of participative management is to empower employees.

5. Participative management develops thinking in terms of ownership at all levels of the company.

6. In participative management, employee goals are aligned with company goals.

7. Change is a constant factor in growth and opportunity.

8. The managerial method of problem solving is:

   A. Identifying the issue

   B. Inventorying assets

   C. Goal setting and goal aligning

   D. Appraising performance

   E. Developing consequences

9. Assessment is basic to effective consultation.

LEADERSHIP BY ENCOURAGEMENT APPLICATIONS

1. Using the characteristics of participative management listed in the chapter, indicate how your company has a participative philosophy and how the philosophy is definitely not participative. Be specific.

2. The case study presented in the chapter is an example of how leadership by encouragement was established in one company. What might the roadblocks and hurdles be in establishing this approach in your company?

ENCOURAGEMENT SKILLS

Participative Management Skills

Participative management develops ownership thinking and participation in decision making and financial gain. There is an attitude of trust, equality, and real involvement. Associates take full responsibility for their actions and the consequences of their actions. The work atmosphere is characterized by risk taking, responsibility, confidence, and feeling that company goals are aligned with individual goals.

Participative management focuses on sharing authority and full involvement as equals. The focus is on encouragement and empowering people. The vision of the leadership is clearly expressed in a dialogue with associates so that common goals are reached. The emphasis is on developing a community of acceptance and belonging with common purposes in terms of work tasks.

Vignette

When participative management was introduced at a local newspaper, it became apparent that two of the senior departmental managers were threatened by the philosophy and process. They believed that everything had been going well and there was no real need for change. They made it clear that they would fight the participative management process in every possible way.

1. What strategy would you use to communicate the participative management philosophy to the resistant managers?

2. What might the advantage of the participative management process be for these managers?

3. What type of training process in participative management would you use when managers appear to be threatened?

4. Develop a systematic plan for installing the participative management process when there appears to be a reasonably high level of acceptance and full support from upper management.

REFERENCES

1. Peters, T., *Thriving on Chaos*, New York: Alfred A. Knopf, 1987.

2. Peters, T. and Waterman, R., *In Search of Excellence: Lessons from America's Best-Run Companies*, New York: Harper & Row, 1982.

3. Waterman, R.H. Jr., *The Renewal Factor*, New York: Bantam Books, 1987.

4. Marsh, W., "The six R's of motivation." *Australian Accountant*, November 1988, pp. 26–29.

5. Kern, R., *Lifestyle Scale*, Coral Springs, FL: CMTI Press, 1990.

6. Wellins, R., "Taking the mystery out of self-directed teams." *Tapping the Network Journal*, Spring/Summer 1991, pp. 19–23.

7. Dinkmeyer, D. and Losoncy, L., *The Encouragement Book: How to Become a Positive Person,* New York: Prentice-Hall, 1980.

8

BUILDING ENCOURAGING
ORGANIZATIONS

"The purpose of organizations is
to help people have lives. Lives come from
the challenges and support that people derive from
being responsible, being supplied, or being cared for."

Philip Crosby

The March 1992 issue of *Fortune* announced two significant additions to the National Business Hall of Fame: the legendary Sam Walton, founder of Wal-Mart, and Max DePree of Herman Miller. These leaders carried their organizations dynamically because of their own personal beliefs in encouragement.

"The people who get on in this world are
the people who get up and look for the circumstances
they want and if they can't find them, make them."

George Bernard Shaw

Sam Walton was characterized as being very close to his employees (whom he called associates). His famous travels throughout the United States to visit his many stores at least once a year indicates the importance he placed on employees. His message clearly was that each employee should develop a supportive, encouraging relationship with the customer.

Max DePree believes that an organization should not merely give benefits to employees. Like Wal-Mart, his company, Herman Miller, is recognized in the *Fortune* survey as "one of America's most admired corporations." DePree's book, *Leadership Is an Art,*[1] communicates that a leader must become "a servant and an encourager." DePree believes in human contact and is quoted as saying that in good leadership, "the touch and the voice must always be connected" and "your behavior must match your beliefs."

As more organizations utilize teams to achieve results, the working environment will change dramatically. In an encouraging, participative work environment, there is continuous learning.[1] The leader no longer makes all the decisions or attempts to manipulate employees to follow. The new organizational leaders are responsible for building organizations in which employees continually expand their capabilities and improve their vision.

In *The Power of Followership*, Robert Kelly states that 80 percent of the success of any project in an organization is based on the followers, and leaders contribute only 20 percent to the success of the project. Kelly believes that exemplary followers are those who think for themselves and are innovative and creative. They give constructive feedback, and they stand up for their beliefs. They are basically committed to the goals of the organization and to making them work. Exemplary leaders have a high level of social interest and a desire to cooperate and work with the organization. They are team players. As a result, they build a network of internal bridges that connect people within the organization. They emphasize equality, mutual respect, and common goals.[2]

MOTIVATION, INVOLVEMENT, AND ORGANIZATIONAL STRUCTURE

Motivation theory indicates that people will be motivated to perform well when the following conditions exist:

1. Rewards are perceived to be tied to *performance*

2. Rewards tied to performance are *valued*

3. Effective performance is perceived to be *achievable*

In an organizational structure with few levels or layers of management, decision making is forced to the lowest possible level. Such organizations are usually divided so that units are responsible for particular products or customers. This enables workers to feel ownership of products or services and to directly service customers.

High-involvement organizations require enthusiastic leaders who energize and support people in self-motivating directions. These leaders help to stimulate a search for the most effective process. They provide essential direction and purpose. They are influential in shaping the culture of the organization. Research by Kotter and Heskett shows a clear link between the value of an organization and its performance. They surveyed 207 major U.S. companies, established a topology of cultures, and correlated these types against financial results in order to quantify the impact of the corporate culture. They found that highly profitable companies such as Pepsico, Wal-Mart, and Shell have adaptive cultures that serve the interests of the customers, employees, and stockholders. They also found that companies that successfully satisfied this triad increased their sales by an average of 682 percent, while companies that satisfied only one or two of these groups increased sales by only 166 percent.[2]

The Conditions of Empowerment

Leaders in an organization need to understand human behavior and motivation if they are to find the fit between the needs and goals of the organization and those of the individual employees. This permits the development of a win–win agreement—a contract between the leader and the employee. When individual and organizational goals are aligned and such agreements are established, there is a clear, mutual understanding of commitment and people are able to motivate and supervise themselves.

Participative Management

Empowerment and involvement are the bases for participative management. Participative management requires a shift in the organizational structure and hierarchy. This is clearly depicted by Plunkett and Fournier:[3]

Traditional Organizational Structure

- Top-down direction is required for control
- Clear signing authority and decision-making levels exist
- Information is restricted to key people
- Specialization is key for job/work design

- Relationships between units need to be managed by appropriate levels
- Bottom of the organization exists to support the top

Participative Management Structure

- Top of organization provides leadership (e.g., vision, goals, support)
- Control is shared with those who influence results
- Decision making is shared on some issues
- Signing authority meets legal requirements instead of operating requirements
- Information is necessary for operations people to do their jobs and make decisions
- Both generalization (i.e., having multiple skills) and specialization are the norm; people do what they need to do
- Relationships between units are managed by those who need to interact
- The top of the organization exists to support the bottom

"The decision we reached around that time, to commit ourselves to giving the associates more equitable treatment in the company, was without a doubt the single smartest move we ever made at Wal-Mart. "

Sam Walton

The Horizontal Organization

Encouragement is a process based on equality. People deal with one another as equals. Hierarchical organizations are no longer appropriate today. Encouraging, empowering, participative, learning organizations are based on high employee involvement and self-managing teams. There is less emphasis on top-down management and more emphasis on the people who do the work managing their own work. There is also emphasis on managing business *processes* rather than just departments. The focus is on relationships rather than status.

This type of organization facilitates encouragement because it values the individual, encourages and supports positive movement, and provides opportunities for employees to improve the workplace.

Losoncy describes a number of techniques for leaders who want to encourage a team approach:

1. ***Team theming*** is the use of collective pronouns such as "we," "our," and "us" rather than "I" or "me."

2. ***Cooperative focusing*** acknowledges and rewards collaboration, in contrast to such typical competitive behaviors as claims of unfairness or favoritism and blaming.

3. ***Welcome-mat weaving*** is recommended to introduce new members or to welcome back old members from vacation, sick leave, or disciplinary leave. It involves sharing mutual interests between veterans and new employees and letting returning employees know that their efforts were missed.

4. ***Team esteeming*** is similar to developing self-esteem; however, the focus is on group efforts. The leader can point out how each person's resources fit into the total team's resources.[4]

TEAM BUILDING: AN INTERPERSONAL SKILLS LEARNING INTERVENTION

> "Teamwork doesn't happen automatically and it doesn't result just from the exhortation of a single leader. It results from members paying attention to how they are working together, identifying issues that block teamwork and working on them; they have to process their group actions. This calls for a collective self-awareness, openness, and maturity that are still not widely found in very many teams in our culture."
>
> Peter Vail

Team building is an organizational intervention which the authors frequently use as consultants. It is used effectively with intact work groups that have some interdependent relationship. It is one of the most powerful interventions that a work group can employ to both foster positive feedback and manage confrontations in specific areas in order to promote empowerment and growth.

The typical format is to meet first with the CEO, president, coordinator, director, etc. Because team-building sessions specifically involve positive and negative feedback directed toward the leader, it is important to coach the leader in receiving feedback at this pre-meeting.

During this meeting, the specific format for asking the same questions to all team members is discussed. Company or work team issues/questions are also added to the general questions.

Then the entire work team is assembled for an orientation to the theory and practice of team building. ("Team-building" by Reilly and Jones[5] is a good reference for the features, advantages, and benefits of team-building sessions.)

In addition to introducing team building as a concept, some initial group activities such as drawing one's family of origin compared to one's current place in the organization (discussed in Chapter 3) are good ways to break the ice.

Group members are told they will be interviewed individually using a standard set of questions that focus on such topics as roles, goals, the job itself, the organization, interpersonal relationships, interpersonal perceptions, the work team, suggested changes, and other issues specific to the team. Each team member is guaranteed anonymity, which means that no response will be attributed to any one person. However, everything that is said is considered team-related business and is thus not confidential.

The interviews are then conducted in a private office; 30 to 45 minutes per person is suggested. During each interview, the consultant takes copious notes to record the exact phrases/language of the team member. After each interview, the interviewee is asked not to talk about the specific questions to other team members so that their responses will be spontaneous and unrehearsed.

At the end of the day, the consultant goes over the notes and writes specific representative responses to each of the above-defined topical areas on large sheets of newsprint.

On day two, the consultant posts all the sheets of newsprint, with each sheet folded in half to prevent participants from reading the data ahead of time. After everyone arrives, the consultant then unfurls the sheets of newsprint to reveal the team data. The rest of the day is then spent discussing/processing the team issues. This is similar to a basic encounter group except that actual team issues are being discussed. The situation can be tense at times as specific frustrations/hurts/resentments, etc. surface, but unexpected positive reactions also emerge.

Intergroup problem solving, confrontation meetings, goal setting and goal alignment, planning sessions, and third-party facilitation are consulting strategies often utilized in team-building sessions. At the end of day two, a series of action steps involving specific individuals who have specific tasks due on specific dates emerge.

Whenever possible, a follow-up session is scheduled for two to four weeks later. Many work teams have annual or semi-annual team-building sessions to facilitate the important interpersonal skills learning component. Thus, a key organizational intervention for the encouraging leader is to periodically utilize team-building sessions with interdependent work groups. It is truly the hallmark of a courageous work team willing to confront both positive and negative perceptions in order to improve relationships and productivity. Feedback is the breakfast of champions.

> "**A** number of those who have written about teams have used the metaphor of a jazz combo or orchestra. In these examples, individual musicians—many with very different talents and playing different instruments—play 'as one.' Teamwork is not optional, but a prerequisite to successful performance. They are led by a leader who coordinates rather than controls, who points the way but does not define it. The individual musicians not only know how to play, they know how to play *together*. Finally, driving each musician's performance is a vision of a given piece that is shared by others. The result is a group performance that is significantly more satisfying than the sum of its individual parts."
>
> Gary Heil, Tom Parker, and Rick Tate
> in *Leadership and the Customer*

Case Study

This case study illustrates how team building and leadership style were addressed at one company by Daniel Eckstein. An outdoor activities center was co-owned by a husband and wife. The company offered dinner cruises, whale-watching trips, surfing, and water skiing, among other water-based recreational activities. The organization was also in the process of adding a Hawaiian luau three nights a week at a resort hotel.

The first intervention consisted of a meeting between the consultant and the husband and wife co-owners. During that meeting, the wife complained that in her role as director of marketing, she reported directly to the president, who also just happened to be her husband. "When we go home, he takes his work with him and still speaks to me like the boss," she commented.

Her husband agreed that this was indeed a problem. He related the stress he felt trying to keep the company financially sound while risking the addition of the luaus to the product line. He also criticized his wife's performance in her capacity as director of marketing.

The first intervention was a structural one involving the dual relationship they had as husband/wife and boss/subordinate. As is often the case in family businesses, the husband and wife each wore two different hats, one at home and one at work. Rather than having appropriately compartmentalized their respective home/work relationships, there was a negative transfer from one to the other. This scenario was vividly portrayed by Robert Duvall in the movie *The Great Santini,* based on the book by Pat Conroy. Duvall played a general who unsuccessfully attempted to autocratically boss his wife and kids at home in a manner similar to his behavior at the base.

The president's discouraging put-downs toward his wife/director of marketing were also confronted. She acknowledged that her performance had dropped but that it was motivated primarily by her feeling of powerlessness. She had translated the disrespect shown by her husband/boss into a revenge-oriented approach to her job. The issue was thus identified as "willingness" with a corresponding "low-task/high-relationship" leadership intervention.

A structural change was made in the wife's organizational position so that she would no longer report directly to her husband. With the coming addition of the luau, she shifted her focus to that part of the business. She was happy to report to the coordinator of that project while concurrently maintaining a good deal of autonomy in her work. Thus, she viewed it as a lateral move that removed her from the direct boss–subordinate relationship with her husband.

They then focused on other organizational challenges. A team-building session (see Chapter 7) was suggested to integrate the luau division into the other established product lines. Several issues surfaced at that meeting. Various members of the established profitable portion of the business were fearful that the luaus were too risky and would bankrupt the company. They were also jealous of what they felt was an inappropriate amount of time the president was devoting to the new luau division.

There were cultural conflicts as well. For example, the captains of the cruise boats were predominately Caucasian males, whereas the leadership and many workers in the luaus were Hawaiian women. The former activity was water based whereas the latter was land based.

Phase 2 of the intervention consisted of an initial team-building session with a series of follow-up sessions with the two groups. The consultant used a specific intervention known as an "image exchange."

The white male cruise boat captains were given three sheets of large newsprint labeled A1 ("how we see us"), A2 ("how we see them)", and A3 ("how we think they see us"). Their task was to go to a separate room and fill out the three sheets of paper.

At the same time, the Hawaiian luau group was also given three sheets of paper with the following headings: B1 ("how we see us"), B2 ("how we see them"), and B3 ("how we think they see us").

Both groups were given 30 minutes to complete the three sheets. When they returned to the common meeting room, the sheets were unfurled and read to the total group by volunteers from each respective subgroup in the following sequence:

1. A1 ("how we see us"), A3 ("how we think they see us"), and B2 ("how we see them")—The three sheets were posted side by side, and similarities and differences were then circled and discussed.

2. B1 ("how we see us"), B3 ("how we think they see us"), and A2 ("how we see them")—Again, the similarities and differences were compared and contrasted.

Key issues of agreement and disagreement were identified. Follow-up meetings to reconcile differences were then utilized. For example, one major perception of the captains by the Hawaiians was that while the men were competent, they were also very arrogant and condescending toward the women. There was also jealousy over salary differences. The captains perceived the Hawaiians as being lazier, less committed to their perception of the Protestant work ethic, and more spiritually oriented.

Follow-up sessions were held in which both groups continued to speak with each other and learn greater appreciation and respect for each other. These were supplemented with consultant-led structured experiences that required intergroup collaborative problem-solving strategies. Each group also attended the other's respective functions (i.e., going on a cruise or attending a luau) as further means of appreciating one another. Brainstorming sessions were used to see how each group could cross-feed customers to the other.

Concurrent with the intergroup problem-solving sessions, the consultant also met with the president to coach him on his leadership style. Several personnel challenges involved the three cruise ship captains. One particularly challenging situation involved a captain who had been with the company for more than ten years, three years longer than the president. The captain continually commented that he thought things were better in the past, and he ignored new policies and procedures, such as documentation for equipment and services.

The president realized that he had basically been ignoring the problem. He was operating in a "low-task/low-relationship," laissez-faire mode. He also became aware of how much he wanted this captain's approval of his leadership style.

First he changed to a more relationship-oriented style, but the results were not satisfactory. The captain interpreted it as a sign of weakness. Even the president's attempts to encourage the captain's strengths were viewed as a sign of weakness. A more directed focus on both the task (i.e., reports not being completed, inadequate ship maintenance, etc.) and the desired relationship still brought no lasting results. Two written warnings were issued. Finally, the president adopted a "get-tough," "do-it-or-else," "high-task/low-relationship" leadership style. With no favorable results forthcoming, the logical consequence of firing the disruptive captain was instituted.

This was difficult for the president because he viewed it as a personal failure. "Termination is a problem-solving strategy, albeit an often undesirable one," the consultant observed. He also reminded the president of how many requests he had made with specific behavioral expectations.

A second leadership challenge involved the director of the luaus. The president felt there was a communication problem between them. The president's style had been to structure the task in early meetings and then wait for her to ask for assistance or clarification. However, in talking with the director of the luaus, the consultant discovered that she took great pride in her work and was thus reluctant to seek the president's advice because she felt it showed weakness on her part. The president's interpretation was that she was doing fine without him. Thus, there was a gap between their styles. The intervention consisted of coaching them on how to better read each other's cues and how to reframe or reinterpret requests for assistance or clarification so as not to indicate incompetence.

These interventions over a three-month period proved to be helpful in assisting the transition to a new product line. After a one-quarter loss, profits surpassed the previous year's high mark. Anonymous employee surveys indicated greater job satisfaction and more confidence in the president's leadership style. The husband/wife co-owners were also happier in their marriage as a result of the change in the structure of their relationship at work.

Gale Forsyth, executive director of organizational learning services at 3M, uses the creative analogy of a hockey team to illustrate what he calls "liberal leadership":

> "Who is the leader on a hockey team? It switches back and forth depending on who has the puck. And where is the ostensible leader, the coach? Sitting on the sideline without skates on. A coach can't tell his skaters where to take that puck, but when the buzzer sounds, it is the team that's out there on the ice.

My role as a coach is about three things. Number One is to give employees the tools they need to do their jobs. I'm not asking you to skate on tennis shoes. I give you skates. If you need a new computer system, my job is to make sure you have it. Number Two is to remove obstacles that hinder team performance. One common obstacle is bureaucracy; nothing clogs a team's arteries faster than bureaucracy. Number Three is to challenge the imagination.

The sum of all the coach's actions is to give the team ownership of the game and build trust. They know the coach isn't going to come out on the ice and tell them how to play the game. But they can report back to me and say, 'I need a new stick,' or 'We have an interpersonal situation here that needs resolution.' The rules of the game are the values that you play by: ethical standards, quality, customer delight. When you win, there's a tremendous feeling of shared accomplishment. It's like winning the Stanley Cup—everyone wins equally."[6]

ENCOURAGEMENT CIRCLES: IMPLEMENTING ENCOURAGEMENT IN THE ORGANIZATION

Encouragement can be impromptu, systematic, or planned. While encouragement is usually given by the leader, encouragement circles provide an opportunity for members to learn the power of encouragement both at work and in their lives. The circles are designed to solve problems, process feedback, and build morale (see Appendix #8, The Encouragement Circle Process).

An encouragement circle is an organized group process in which six to eight people work together to learn to become more encouraging to themselves and others. Participation is voluntary, and the group is concerned with the development of each member's self-esteem and desire to cooperate.

Encouragement circles are concerned with the total person. Therefore, any concerns or challenges, whether on or off the job, that the group feels comfortable with and capable of dealing with can be discussed. The major focus, however, is on work-related issues and problem solving through encouragement. The group serves to enhance learning through both instructional and experiential methods. Each member learns to investigate his or her own beliefs, attitudes, values, and goals.

The group's objectives are:

1. To enable all members to increase their self-esteem

2. To help members become aware of the power and satisfaction available when they implement their choices

3. To increase the social interest or cooperation and caring of each person in order to improve interpersonal relationships

4. To develop a cooperative relationship between management and staff and thus promote a feeling of "we" and "us" instead of "they" and "them"

5. To build team spirit

6. To learn to explore all possible solutions

7. To become aware that the encouragement process can be applied to all of life's challenges

8. To increase the quality of work life, reduce stress and tension, promote greater job satisfaction, increase involvement and participation in the problem-solving process, and open communication at all levels

Although group membership is voluntary, encouragement circles need to be supported at all levels of the organization. Management and employees alike need to believe in the groups, lend support, and, when possible, become totally involved. It is important to get key employees involved in encouragement circles from the start.

The leader of the group should be someone who is perceived as unbiased toward either management or staff on major issues. This person needs to be someone who is respected and who can develop mutual respect. The leader needs communication skills, leadership skills, and knowledge of group dynamics and methods of processing feedback, all of which can be acquired by reading, studying, and practicing.

Training also can be provided by consultants who are specialists in leadership by encouragement and who can model the process. Specific sessions may be devoted to group leadership, the group process and group dynamics, and methods for facilitating interaction and problem solving.

Responsibilities of the leader include:

1. Schedule group meetings according to time constraints of members

2. Create a safe environment in which people feel free to share their feelings and opinions (the importance of confidentiality is stressed at the first meeting as members agree to keep confidential any personal information discussed in the group)

3. Process information from the group by utilizing group leadership skills

4. Keep the group focused on the encouragement approach

Format of the Encouragement Circle

1. In the first session, the leader clarifies the objectives and purposes of the group. The group is expected to do some reading to promote skill development.

   The leader clearly states the purpose of the group so that everyone understands what will and will not be discussed. It is important for members to understand that the purpose of the group is to provide an opportunity to share problems and process feedback. The group is not a gripe session in which people complain but nothing is resolved. The emphasis is on problem solving through encouragement. If the group digresses from its basic purpose, the leader asks the group to consider how the current discussion relates to its purpose.

2. Introductions enable members to become better acquainted. Each person states his or her name and says something about why he or she wants to be part of the group. The leader begins the exercise by modeling a personal statement in being congruent, open, and honest, such as "I am interested in being in this group to understand what motivates me and how to work more effectively with people." The leader also helps to clarify any confusion about the purpose of the group.

3. Group members share two things they like about themselves.

4. The leader discusses how encouragement can be both verbal and nonverbal. The leader indicates a number of nonverbal ways to discourage, such as certain looks, and how one can encourage with a smile or a touch.

5. Group members are asked to circulate, encourage others nonverbally, and, at the leader's signal, pick a partner.

6. Each partner shares three personal strengths and then describes the most encouraging person in his or her life and some specific traits of that person.

7. These traits are then shared with the entire group in order to identify what an encouraging person actually does. The traits can be listed on a board or newsprint.

8. Groups of two then form foursomes, introduce one another in terms of strengths, and talk about ways to maintain and develop a positive outlook on work and life.

This introductory session may well take up all of the first meeting. As time permits, however, the leader will want to select one concern and lead a sample discussion to demonstrate how the group might use the encouragement process to work through that concern.

The method for discussing concerns consists of the five steps described below. It is important to follow the format systematically in early meetings until the group becomes familiar with the process.

The Encouragement Circle Process

1. Listen to feelings and beliefs, avoid "shoot and reload" dialogues, and be empathic, which does not necessarily mean agreeing with the speaker.

2. Identify the real issue, which may be control, perfectionism, pleasing, victim, martyr, superiority, comfort, getting attention, or power.

3. Inventory the individual's assets, strengths, possibilities, and potential for dealing with the challenge or the real issue, including those areas where the person functions well. The group is asked to brainstorm about the individual's strengths in dealing with the issue. The group also can help the person become aware of how he or she may be contributing to the problem.

4. The leader teaches the group how to develop perceptual alternatives, or other positive ways of looking at or understanding the situation.

5. The person is encouraged to develop an active, constructive approach to the challenge and to make a commitment to change.

After the encouragement process has been explained, the group selects one concern or challenge and deals with it according to this format. Here, the emphasis is on being empathic, identifying real issues, and being encouraging. Depending on the group's level of sophistication, the leader may need to provide some additional practice in specific encouragement skills.

At the end of the session, group members are encouraged to share what they have learned and their specific plans and commitments for the next session. Each member completes the following sentences: "I learned or I relearned that…" and "This week, I will…"

Ensuing sessions begin with members sharing their successes in being encouraged and discussing challenges when they have not felt successful. The group learns to give feedback to each member.

As members of the group suggest problems or challenges, the group selects a problem on which to focus. In any problem or challenge, it is important for the group to identify something that may appear unique to one person but has many common components from which all can learn.

Skills to be developed include:

1. Attend to one another's communication

2. Listen without judging

3. Respond to one another's concerns instead of refocusing the group on one's own issue

4. Develop responsibility and productivity by focusing on the efforts, resources, and assets of others and by holding people responsible without blame

5. Develop greater respect by conveying confidence in the abilities of others, focusing on their interests, promoting their progress, and cooperating instead of competing

6. Develop a sense of humor and the ability to see oneself in perspective

7. Develop skills to help others overcome their discouraging ideas, beliefs, and attitudes

8. Develop skills in establishing both short- and long-range goals

As group members work on these skills, they become more motivated and more cooperative. They increase their self-esteem and gain a positive attitude. They take full responsibility for their own actions and eliminate excuses and blaming. They increase self-respect, enthusiasm, and energy. They learn to find positive perceptual alternatives and combat irrational beliefs or demands.

The encouragement group supports and validates its members as acceptable human beings. It develops strong motivation. Members learn that they can belong by participating, supporting, and encouraging. As they learn to recognize their own destructive beliefs as well as those of others, group members realize that they can choose positive beliefs. They learn to appreciate the importance of their own expectations and the performance of others.

The goal of encouragement circles is for members to both learn to encourage one another and themselves as well as apply the encouragement process to those outside the circle. In this way, the circle is expanded to touch others.

SUMMARY

The central theme of this chapter is building an encouraging organizational environment. Encouragement is one of the subtle concepts that separates excellence from mediocrity. The organizations and leaders that survive the current challenging economic times will be those that actively promote human relations training activities.

KEY POINTS

1. Leadership by encouragement is a process that focuses on developing an encouraging organization.

2. Participative leadership is one characteristic of the most successful organizations.

3. Participative leadership maximizes both team and individual power.

4. Encouragement circles are a specific example of an organizational commitment to encouragement.

ENCOURAGEMENT SKILLS

1. Seeking feedback is a core skill of leadership by encouragement. Using the list of ten recommendations on pages 221–222, develop a questionnaire for your employees. Have them rate each item on a scale of 1 to 10 (1 = low, 10 = high) and then ask for specific written feedback/suggestions for improvement. Anonymous feedback is suggested to promote candor.

2. Circulate a summary of the findings. Then demonstrate the skill of facilitating encouragement circles by involving your team in both personal encouragement and joint brainstorming/problem-solving activities.

REFERENCES

1. DePree, M., *Leadership Is an Art,* New York: Dell Trade Paperback, 1989.

2. Kelly, R., *The Power of Followership,* New York: Doubleday, 1992.

3. Plunkett, L. and Fournier, R., *Participative Management: Implementing Empowerment,* New York: John Wiley & Sons, 1991.

4. Losoncy, L., *The Motivating Team Leader,* Delray Beach, FL: St. Lucie Press, 1995.

5. Reilly, A. and Jones, J., "Team-building." *The 1974 Handbook for Group Facilitators,* San Diego: University Associates, 1974, pp. 227–237.

6. Champy, J., *Reengineering Management,* New York: Harper Collins, 1995, pp. 134–135.

AFTERWORD

"Change and constant improvement (Kaizen, per the Japanese), the watchwords of the 80's, are no longer enough. Not even close. Only revolution, and perpetual revolution at that, will do."

Tom Peters

We conclude by returning to where we began, defining and illustrating the philosophy and the principles of encouragement. Throughout this book, we have stressed that encouragement is both an *attitude* as well as a set of specific *techniques*. We have also suggested that there is a *theoretical basis* by providing the psychological framework of Alfred Adler and Rudolf Dreikurs related to the practical application of encouragement. We also presented Sam Walton, Jack Welch, and Max DePree as contemporary organizational role models.

"I believe that we have only just begun the process of inventing the new organizational forms that will inhabit the twenty-first century. To be responsible inventors and discoverer though, we need the courage to let go of the old world, to relinquish most of what we have cherished, to abandon our interpretations about what does and doesn't work. We must learn to see the world anew."

Margaret Wheatley

213

We proposed the improving management performance cycle as a developmental model for leaders and presented a discussion of encouragement training and encouraging approaches to performance appraisal.

Each chapter ended with a summary of key points, applications of encouragement skills, and specific action steps for leaders to implement on the job. Throughout the book we have attempted to balance our own ideas about encouragement with relevant research and insights from other professional colleagues.

> "**R**espect, loyalty, security, dignity—old-fashioned qualities for a new-fashioned economy. Earlier this century machines helped liberate our ancestors from the toil of the fields. In this generation, wondrous technology has freed us from the drudgery of the assembly line and enabled us to speed new products to far-off markets. As we approach the millennium, it is people who will carry us forward. In an economy built on service, the extent to which we prosper will depend on our ability to educate, entertain, empower and ennoble ourselves—and each other.
>
> *Fortune*

We have also attempted to provide concrete case studies and examples that bring to life a concept that most leaders espouse but too few actually practice. We welcome comments regarding your own ideas and applications of the principles of encouragement in your organization.

> "**T**he future belongs to
> those who believe in the beauty of their dreams."
>
> Eleanor Roosevelt

To encourage requires a subtle shift in focus in a work environment in which people are too often bombarded with information about shortcomings and the deficiencies of their parents, their culture, their organization, and, of course, themselves. Mafu, a philosopher and spiritual teacher, poignantly illustrates the perceptual shift to encouragement: "If one's primary focus is on the manure pile, he or she will ultimately turn over flowers that 'get in the way' because one is only looking for the manure."

> "**T**he significant problems we face cannot be solved at
> the same level of thinking we were at when we created them."
>
> Albert Einstein

The encouraging leader has the ability to perceive a spark of potential in all employees and then to act as a mirror which reflects that strength or potential back to them. This is a remarkably distinguishing characteristic of great leadership. Such leaders help to translate dreams into reality. The greatest leaders are the ones who inspire us to seek more of life, the ones who help us to remember our dreams, and the ones who touch our hearts with an ability to see the good in all things.

> "I stand up on my desk to remind myself that we must constantly look at things in a different way. You see, the world looks very different from up here. Just when you think you know something you have to look at it in another way. Even though it may seem silly or wrong, you must try. When you read, don't just consider what the author thinks; consider what you think. Boys, you must strive to find your own voice because the longer you wait to begin, the less likely you will find it at all. Thoreau said, 'Most men lead lives of great desperation.' Don't be resigned to that. Break out! Don't just walk off the edge like lemmings, look around you...Dare to strike out and find new ground."
>
> Robin Williams as Professor Keating,
> in *Dead Poets Society*

Encouraging leaders also touch our hearts, as so aptly described in *Managing from the Heart*:[1]

> **H**ear and understand me.
>
> **E**ven if you disagree, don't make me wrong.
>
> **A**cknowledge the greatness within me.
>
> **R**emember to look for my loving intentions.
>
> **T**ell me the truth with compassion.

To lead by encouragement is truly to be the heroic transformational visionary described in *Leadership and the Customer Revolution* as someone who:

- Deals in transformational change

- Adopts the highest of values and is committed to these values even in the face of adversity

- Overcomes a number of substantial obstacles that threaten his or her ability to create the desired changes

- Deals effectively with uncertainty

- Rarely works alone

- Is values driven

- Is persistent even in the face of extreme skepticism

- Thinks differently

- Creates a different sense of order

- Is internally driven and seems relatively unaffected by external rewards, threats, or punishments[2]

Successful encouragement is an emotional experience that translates into cognitive decisions. To encourage is to realize that although there are negative and positive emotions, ultimately it is one's own perception that makes a profound difference in one's view of, response to, and approach to life. Encouragement is one of the practical building blocks that can help bridge the gap between our potential and our self-imposed limitations.

"If you can dream it, you can do it.
Always remember that this whole thing
was started by a mouse."

Walt Disney

REFERENCES

1. Bracey, H., Rosenblum, J., Sanford, A., and Trueblood, R., *Managing from the Heart,* New York: Delacorte, 1990.

2. Heil, G. and Parker, T., *Leadership and the Customer Revolution,* New York: Van Nostrand Reinhold, 1995.

APPENDIX

INTRODUCTION

Practical instruments and handouts for implementing leadership by encouragement are provided in the following activities. These materials have been used in developing leadership by encouragement programs in business, industry, and other organizations. They enable the leader to present the theory, practices, and skills in a simple, cogent fashion.

- ***Encouragement*** is applied to a variety of leadership challenges.

- Leaders are provided with a ***language of encouragement*** to implement the philosophy.

- A method for ***assessing oneself as an encouraging leader*** is included.

- The ***encouraging approach to management*** is set forth in nine essential points.

- The encouraging leader focuses on finding solutions. A five-step method for ***processing solutions*** is provided.

- The ***encouragement circle*** is a unique team-building process which focuses on assets, resources, perceptual alternatives, and active–constructive approaches to challenging situations.

- ***Introduction to the encouragement group*** is an outline for establishing leadership by encouragement classes. It is used with *The Skills of Encouragement*.*

- The ***encouragement training*** materials describe and identify the goals and skills of encouragement training.

- ***Building self-esteem through encouragement skills*** is a set of exercises and group-building materials designed to foster self-esteem and a positive approach, which undergird encouragement.

- The ***performance review*** exemplifies a focus on the positive in a performance review.

- ***Self-evaluation and assessment*** is a format used in the evaluation of staff.

- ***Asset-focusing*** develops the encouragement process by focusing on strengths, resources, and assets of the individual. This section helps the leader to become more aware of each person's potential.

- ***Participative management*** is a process for evaluating the participative management process in an organization.

---

* Dinkmeyer, D. and Losoncy, L., *The Skills of Encouragement: Bringing Out the Best in Yourself and Others,* Delray Beach, FL: St. Lucie Press, 1996.

1. LEADERSHIP BY ENCOURAGEMENT

Basic Philosophy

1. People are the most underdeveloped resource of a company. Encouraged persons have self-esteem, are cooperative, and want to be productive.

2. Productivity is increased by systematically obtaining and using the ideas of workers at every level.

3. The effective leader is a facilitator who creates situations whereby employees can grow, contribute, and produce.

4. Excellence comes from clear goals, decisions by consensus so all participate fully, and decisive action. Each person is fully responsible for his or her actions and results.

5. People are motivated by their goals and a feeling of belonging. As employee goals are aligned with company goals to create a community of acceptance and belonging, destructive tension is reduced and productivity increased.

Psychology of Encouragement

1. We choose, decide, and act in terms of our goals and purpose. Goals are the final explanation for all behavior.

2. Belonging is basic for the individual and for stimulating organizational growth.

3. We seek to move from a less significant position to a position in which we are recognized and valued.

4. Behavior is a result of the perception or meaning we give all our experiences.

5. Discouraged people lack self-esteem and a desire to cooperate. They believe they cannot be successful by contributing and therefore resort to passive, destructive ways of relating. They doubt their abilities. They are characterized by focus on external control and evaluation, unrealistic standards, and emphasis on personal gain.

6. Encouraging leaders:
   A. Identify the positive potential in every situation
   B. Give recognition through positive feedback
   C. Move from power over others to empowering others

Encouraging Leadership Practices

In participative management, all participants are equal in the process. Encouraging leaders and associates:

1. See situations as challenges and opportunities instead of problems—They model positive behavior. They work together to draw out one another's potential and resources. They empower others.

2. Identify the positive and potential in every person and every situation by listening, observing movement, and emphatically reflecting the message so the meaning is understood—They focus on assets, resources, and efforts.

3. Respect individuality and identify similarities—They value uniqueness and find ways to use it in the corporation. They help people recognize and benefit from their similarities.

4. Respond and communicate congruently—They say what they mean and mean what they say. They use "I" messages to communicate positive and negative observations. They use the power of positive feedback. They give specific, timely, and personal recognition.

5. Delegate responsibility—They provide opportunity to make decisions and are held accountable for results. Each person has clear goals, roles, and responsibilities and takes full responsibility for his or her actions and results.

6. Provide positive performance reviews.

Systematic encouragement is not incidental, but rather is part of the leadership plan. Participative management includes:

A. Intervening in negative behaviors

B. Regular brainstorming sessions, collective thinking, and collective responsibility

C. Individual affirmation and visualization

The Skills of Encouragement

1. Listening to meanings and feelings; being present

2. Responding reflectively to indicate understanding

3. Being enthusiastic about the messages and meanings others convey; expecting the positive

4. Focusing on strengths, assets, and resources

5. Developing perceptual alternatives or seeking alternative meanings

6. Being able to see oneself and situations in perspective; having a sense of humor

7. Focusing on efforts and contributions

8. Identifying and combating discouraging fictional beliefs

9. Encouraging commitment and movement toward the other person's goals and helping align them with the goals of the organization

10. Encouraging mutual feedback

2. THE ENCOURAGEMENT PROCESS

The encouragement process is applied in processing various leadership challenges.

1. Present the challenge:
   A. Listen to feelings and beliefs
   B. Respond with understanding to those feelings
   C. Identify the basic concern

2. Identify the real issue:
   A. Is it skill (e.g., ability, knowledge, competence)?
   B. Is it motivation (e.g., control, pleasing, power, revenge)?
   C. Is it a combination of skills and motivation?

3. Inventory the individual's and the company's assets, strengths, efforts, possibilities, and potential resources

4. Develop alternate meanings and options through creative brainstorming prior to action

5. Develop an action plan:
   A. Obtain a commitment to change
   B. Align the personal plan with organizational goals

6. Evaluate using the positive in a performance review format

7. Implement the consequences (e.g., encourage, praise, reprimand)

3. THE SPECIAL LANGUAGE OF ENCOURAGEMENT

When comments about people's efforts are in order, we must be very careful not to place value judgments on what they have done. Too often, we make positive comments in a praising manner, thus expressing our values and opinions rather than helping people believe in themselves.

Encouraging leaders work to eliminate value-loaded words, such as "good," "great," and "excellent," from their vocabularies at these moments. They substitute words of praise with phrases that express the special meaning of encouragement.

Phrases that demonstrate acceptance:

"I like the way you handled that."

"I like the way you tackle a problem."

"I'm glad you're pleased with it."

"Since you're not satisfied, what could you do to be pleased with it?"

"It looks as if you enjoyed that."

"How do you feel about it?"

Phrases that show confidence:

"Knowing you, I'm sure you'll do fine."

"You'll make it!"

"I have confidence in your judgment."

"That's a rough one, but I'm sure you'll work it out."

"You'll figure it out."

Phrases that focus on contributions, assets, and appreciation:

"Thanks, that helped a lot."

"It was thoughtful of you to...."

"I really appreciate...because it makes my job much easier."

"I need your help on...."

Phrases that specifically recognize effort and improvement:

"It looks as if you really worked hard on that."

"It looks as if you spent a lot of time thinking that through."

"I see you're moving along."

"Look at the progress you've made in...."

"You're improving in...."

"You may not feel you've reached your goal, but look how far you've come!"

4. ASSESSING ENCOURAGING LEADERS: YOU AS AN ENCOURAGING MANAGER

The leader meets with supervisors to help them assess their own encouraging behaviors through the following questions:

1. Do you feel it is your responsibility to help develop your subordinates?

2. Do you have a plan for identifying the positive in every person?

3. Are you an attentive listener?

4. Do you respond to the feelings of employees in an empathic way? Can you put their feelings and thoughts into words so they feel understood? Do you hear their message and clearly indicate what you hear?

5. Do you respect your employees' ideas even though you may not think they are as good as yours?

6. Do you understand your employees' concerns and communicate this understanding to them?

7. Are you enthusiastic when you recognize and respond to employees?

8. Do you focus on your employees' strengths and resources?

9. Do you find alternatives for solving problems presented to you?

10. Do you recognize and focus on enthusiasm, effort, and participation?

11. Do you take a positive attitude on most issues and set an example?

12. Do you encourage participation as equals in the managerial process?

13. Do you provide honest and open feedback?

14. Do you give credit where it is due?

5. EVALUATING YOUR LEADERSHIP RELATIONSHIPS

Everyone needs:

1. ***Belonging and love, acceptance, a sense that others care***
   - Do your associates feel belonging and acceptance?

2. ***Power and respect for their opinions*** (this is not the same as acceptance)
   - Do your associates feel important when they are with you?
   - Do you respect their skills and competencies?
   - Do you give them recognition?

3. ***Fun, a sense of humor, a sense of perspective***
   - Do your associates enjoy being at work?
   - Do they perceive you as having a sense of humor and a sense of perspective?

4. ***Freedom***
   - Are your associates allowed to make decisions?
   - Do they feel independent and responsible?

5. ***Purpose and goal accomplishment***
   - Do your associates move toward the group goals as well as their individual goals?

6. ***Encouragement***
   - Do your associates feel appreciated, valued, and involved?
   - Do you recognize your associates for their progress?
   - Are your associates' courageous and risk-taking behaviors increasing?

7. ***To feel significant, recognized for their own unique ways***
   - Do your people feel pride, accomplishment, and worth in the work process?
   - How are you meeting your associates' specific needs?
   - Which associates meet these needs for you?

6. THE ENCOURAGING APPROACH TO MANAGEMENT

Encouraging leaders:

1. See situations as challenges and opportunities instead of problems.

2. Identify the positive and potential in every person and every situation. This is done by listening, observing movement, and responding empathically. Focus on any assets, resources, or potential efforts.

3. Respect individuality and identify similarities.

4. Give recognition. Use the power of positive feedback. Are specific and timely. Personalize and individualize.

5. Respond and communicate congruently. Say what they mean and mean what they say.

6. Develop and encourage responsibility in others. Stimulate their enthusiasm.

7. Provide positive performance reviews.

8. Participate as equals in the process.

9. Ask the following basic questions: What is being encouraged? Who needs to be encouraged?

7. PROCESSING SOLUTIONS: THE IMPROVING MANAGEMENT PERFORMANCE CYCLE

The following simple, effective method tends to improve leadership performance. Whenever a problem is presented, take the following steps in the improving management performance cycle:

1. Issue identification—Get the clear facts and decide exactly what the concern is as opposed to the symptoms. It is important to identify the priorities of the employees and what appears to be important to them, such as getting their way, being in control, or being right.

The Kern Lifestyle Scale is especially helpful in identifying the priorities of employees. It is efficient because it can be taken and scored in minutes. The Lifestyle Scale then identifies such factors as:

1. Control

2. Perfectionism

3. Need to please

4. Victim

5. Martyr

2. Asset inventory—Look for the positive, regardless of the situation. Begin to look at everything in terms of what's good, alright, or positive about it. In this situation, employees can be helped to identify their own strengths and assets; you, of course, can add to these lists of assets.

3. Goal setting and goal aligning—It is important at this point to establish performance standards that are clear, achievable, and realistic and that will secure the involvement of the employee. The leader then needs to identify how the goals of the employee can be aligned with the goals of the organization.

4. Performance appraisal—Once the goals have been established and the projects begin, it is important to systematically and effectively observe, evaluate, and give feedback on performance and progress. Leaders don't just occasionally observe what is happening; they have a clear picture of systematic progress.

5. Consequences—A variety of logical consequences result from employee performance. Often an employee functions effectively, allowing the leader to encourage or point out any progress made.

When there is outstanding performance, the employee, obviously, will be praised. However, when an employee makes a mistake or does not function effectively, you as the leader should advise him or her that there will be immediate feedback. Confirm the fact that the employee has failed to function effectively. Be specific about what was anticipated and what actually happened. Keep your response brief and to the point, and remember to criticize the behavior, not the person. "I" messages are very helpful: "I feel...when...because...." (For example, "I feel very disappointed when you do not reach the quota because I thought we had planned a way this could happen.")

The steps that can be recycled are:

A. Identify the issue.

B. Clarify whether the problem lies in skill or motivation.

C. Identify specific motivational components.

D. Identify what assets are available.

E. Make an appraisal of performance in a clear, effective manner.

Participative management is a human relations approach to leadership which is built upon a solid set of psychological concepts and methods. A managerial method for resolving conflict and moving toward cooperation and productivity is basic to implementing change. Human resource departments and business and organizational consultants trained in psychology put such programs into action.

8. THE ENCOURAGEMENT CIRCLE PROCESS

The encouragement circle process* includes the following steps:

1. Listen to feelings and beliefs. Be empathic while identifying feelings and beliefs.

2. Identify the real issue, which may be control, perfectionism, victim, martyr, superiority, comfort, pleasing, power, revenge, or seeking to display inadequacy.
    A. Identify a specific situation.
    B. Tell what happened.
    C. Relate how you felt.

3. Inventory the individual's assets, strengths, possibilities, and potential for dealing with the challenge. Identify other challenges of living where that person is functioning effectively (e.g., where he or she handles power effectively).

4. Develop perceptual alternatives, or other positive ways to understand the situation.

5. Develop an active–constructive approach to the challenge and a specific commitment to change.

At the end of each session, group members are asked to share what they have learned and their specific plan or commitment for the following week. Each member completes the following statements:

"I learned..."

"This week I will..."

Ensuing sessions begin by sharing successes the members had in being encouraging and discussing challenges when they did not feel successful.

The encouragement group provides support and validation. Members learn they belong by participating, supporting, and encouraging. They learn to focus on the positive.

---

* Dinkmeyer, D. and Losoncy, L., *The Skills of Encouragement: Bringing Out the Best in Yourself and Others,* Delray Beach, FL: St. Lucie Press, 1996.

9. INTRODUCTION TO THE ENCOURAGEMENT GROUP

Classroom atmosphere and feedback

Goals:

1. To listen in an encouraging way

2. To affirm and encourage yourself and others

3. To focus on strengths and resources

4. To deal with discouragement positively

5. To see positive alternatives in the decision-making process and increase one's ability to see such possibilities

6. To become more courageous

7. To focus on the strengths, resources, and efforts of others

Encouragement is the process of focusing on resources in order to build one's self-esteem and self-confidence. Encouragers:

1. Focus on internal, not external, control

2. Seek internal, not external, evaluation

3. Recognize effort and progress without requiring completion

4. See the positive, are accepting, and have faith in the person

Exercises:

1. Each group member lists three things he or she likes about himself or herself. Ask each person to consider the following:

   A. How much time have you spent this week doing something positive and beneficial?

   B. Do you usually reach your goals or make little progress toward reaching them?

   C. What is your claim to fame? How do you seek to be known? What is your reputation in that area?

2. Each group member lists five characteristics of the most encouraging person in his or her life. The group compiles these characteristics to create a master description of an encourager.

3. Each group member lists five characteristics of the most discouraging person in his or her life. The group compiles these characteristics to create a master description of a discourager.

It's up to you whether you choose encouragement or intimidation as an interpersonal style.

10. ENCOURAGEMENT TRAINING

Developing an organization that functions in an encouraging manner does not happen by chance. It requires goals, planning, modeling, training, and the observation and recognition of encouraging behavior. Members transfer their self-esteem to pride in the value and worth of the organization. They receive belonging, cooperation, and mutual goal alignment.

Goals:

- Positive self-awareness
- Positive self-esteem
- Self-determination
- Self-motivation
- Positive expectations of oneself
- Positive self-image
- Goal orientation

Encouragement Training: A Competency-Based Program

I. Improving Relationships through Communication
   A. Attending
      1. Maintain eye contact
      2. Keep alert posture
      3. Stay on the topic
   B. Listening
      1. Focus on feelings, concerns, and beliefs
      2. Remain nonjudgmental
   C. Responding
      1. Give open, not closed, responses
      2. Avoid "shoot and reload" dialogue
      3. Demonstrate understanding of the message
   D. Showing empathy
      1. Communicate feelings and beliefs

II. Developing encouragement skills
   A. Increasing responsibility
      1. Focus on efforts and contributions
      2. Recognize resources and potential
      3. Expect people to be responsible without blaming them
   B. Improving productivity
      1. Examine whether your leadership reduces productivity
      2. Examine whether your leadership increases productivity

C. Developing communication of respect for others
   1. Share positive expectations
   2. Express confidence in people
   3. Recognize their claims to fame
   4. Focus on their interests
D. Building cooperation
   1. Cooperate with others
   2. Avoid competing
   3. Build mutual respect
   4. Recognize the value of differences and uniqueness
E. Identifying similarities
   1. Build interconnectedness
   2. Increase connections
   3. Develop a feeling of "we-ness"
F. Finding humor in situations
G. Assisting others in overcoming their discouraging ideas
   1. Identify negative beliefs
   2. Deal with negative behaviors
H. Establishing short- and long-range goals
I. Mutually evaluating progress
J. Developing enthusiasm
K. Developing perceptual alternatives
L. Focusing on efforts and contributions
M. Finding strengths, assets, and potential
N. Encouraging commitment and movement
O. Becoming self-encouraging

11. BUILDING SELF-ESTEEM THROUGH ENCOURAGEMENT SKILLS

Identifying Personal Strengths and Resources

The goal is to know what is positive about yourself. Recognizing, identifying, and sharing your strengths are the basis for increasing your self-confidence and developing your skill as an encourager.

This exercise helps to create an awareness of your personal strengths and develops in you the courage to become more self-appreciative and to experience more self-confidence.

  A. Identify three of your personal strengths or resources. These are traits or abilities you feel positive about.

  B. Share these resources with a partner. Have your partner share three strengths and resources with you. If you feel self-conscious about sharing, understand that it is not bragging or competing, but recognizing and owning your strengths.

  C. How do you presently use your resources personally and professionally? Indicate ways in which these resources are used regularly in your life. Have your partner share his or her use of resources.

  D. How could you increase the use of your resources?

Taking More Responsibility for Your Self-Esteem and Your Emotional State

When you are willing to take charge of your mental and physical resources (your emotional state), you are then taking greater responsibility for how you feel about yourself. It is important to begin by becoming aware of your present state. Are you feeling positive, enthused, and energized or negative, apathetic, and discouraged?

Be aware of your capacity to be in charge of your state. Think of times when you felt positive and enthused. How did you get to that state? Was it something you said to yourself or something you heard?

We are all triggered by situations in our lives. You can use any experience to put yourself into a discouraging or encouraging state. It has a lot to do with the way you breathe and relax, with your ability to see positive situations, and what you tell yourself.

You can experiment with being in charge of your state. One way to establish a positive state is through self-affirmation. Self-affirmation moves away from negative self-talk to positive self-talk. You can do this by identifying some statements about yourself that are self-affirming (for example, "I believe in myself," "I am responsible," "I like myself," "I can see the positive in any situation"). There are obviously many other statements you could make, based upon your beliefs and your positive perceptions.

You self-affirm by the following steps:

A. Relax your body by sitting with both feet on the floor, with your hands in your lap.

B. Close your eyes. Breathe deeply through your nose. Say self-affirming sentences. You can practice self-affirmation regularly, thereby building your self-confidence and your ability to be in charge of your state.

C. Develop the ability to listen and understand feelings. By responding empathically to feelings, you eventually elicit and encourage others to express their feelings. Choose a partner and begin by talking about some emotions and feelings you are having now. Have your partner listen closely and indicate the feelings he or she heard by saying, "You are angry, upset, happy, annoyed." Then have your partner share; indicate what you have heard.

   Recognize that as you learn how to understand and empathize with feelings, others will relate more effectively with you.

D. Expand your capacity to focus on your assets and resources. To expand your awareness, open your mind and perceptions to any possible asset you have in a situation. It may be physical, social, emotional, or psychological. To expand your awareness of these assets, consider the following:

   • Health
   • Self-confidence
   • Sociability
   • Sense of humor
   • Patience
   • Empathy
   • Perspective

Indicate how you can presently use these assets.

E. Develop your capacity to perceive possibilities instead of limitations and to be flexible and creative. You can take any situation and turn it from a negative into a positive. Positive learning can come from any experience. A negative trait may have some positive potential when seen from a different perspective (e.g., stubborn becomes determined, demanding becomes persistent, aggressive becomes energetic).

Discuss some personal situations with friends or loved ones in whom you see negative traits. Find out whether your partner can identify the positive sides of these particular traits.

Focusing on Efforts and Contributions

We tend to live in situations in which we only reward or recognize full efforts. However, this limits the motivation of individuals who are not at the moment producing a full effort. We need to know how to motivate those who are making minimal efforts but are making progress. Often we are better at finding fault than finding the positive. In the following exercise, continue to see the positive potential in any situation.

With your partner, identify some situations where people are making little effort. Can you identify any positive movement?

Take charge of your own perception of success. One way to do this is to be in charge of your own standards. Develop your ability to set standards which create a feeling of success for you and which do not require you to regularly compete with others.

If you are involved in athletics or exercise, recognize any movement or progress you make. If you are learning a new skill, for example in music, dance, or some other artistic area, recognize any sign of improvement.

12. PERFORMANCE REVIEW

Name:_____   Self-Evaluation Date: _____

1. Current job (job description and expectations of employer/supervisor)

   _____

   _____

2. What is going well? What has been accomplished? _____

   _____

   _____

3. What needs improvement? _____

   _____

   _____

4. Supervisor Evaluation

   Strengths, assets, things going well:_____

   _____

   _____

   Things that require improvement: _____

   _____

   _____

   Agreed-upon plans for improvement: _____

   _____

   _____

5. Mutually achievable goals: _____

   _____

   _____

13. SELF-EVALUATION AND ASSESSMENT

Name:_____   Position:_____

Marital Status: _____

Children: _____

Professional goals and expectations:
Satisfaction at tasks (on scale of 1 to 10, 1 = low, 10 = high):

_____	Work	_____	Self
_____	Friendship	_____	Leisure
_____	Opposite sex	_____	Parenting

Strengths:

_____

_____

_____

Family constellation:

_____

_____

_____

Ratings	*Highest*	*Lowest*
Intelligence	_____	_____
Achievement	_____	_____
Responsibility	_____	_____
Rebelliousness	_____	_____
Trying to please	_____	_____

Ratings	Highest	Lowest
Sense of humor	_____	_____
Sensitivity	_____	_____
Who is most different from you?	_____	_____
Who is most like you?	_____	_____

Early recollections:

_____

_____

_____

14. ASSET-FOCUSING

Leaders are often limited because they focus on liabilities and mistakes. Their pessimistic, negative focusing builds negative self-image.

You can encourage anyone by focusing on assets. We have a choice about what we focus on and perceive.

In *The Motivating Leader*, Lewis Losoncy* developed the concept of asset-focusing. When we look at people, we need to be aware of a broad range of potential assets. As Losoncy indicates:

> "**A**sset-focusing involves being tuned in to observing 'what is right with' or 'what is a potential resource of another person.' Asset-focusing is an approach to help re-image an individual into a more positive self-image. Asset-focusing is a leader's way of building by constructing. How could you as a leader make use of asset-focusing in your organization?"

The following list is an adaptation of Losoncy's lengthier list:

accepting	charitable	determined	growing
accessible	clarifier	diligent	happy
accommodating	competent	easy-going	healthy
achieving	comprehensive	energetic	honest
action-oriented	concise	enlightening	hope-giving
adaptable, flexible	confident	enterprising	humorous
ambitious	congenial	enthusiastic	imaginative
amenable	conscientious	ethical	impartial
amusing	cooperative	exhaustive	improving
approachable	cordial	expedient	improvising
assertive	courageous	explicit	independent
assiduous,	creative	faithful	indispensable
hard-working	credible	forgiving	individualistic
astute	critical	frank	industrious
attentive	curious	fun-loving	ingenious
authentic	decisive	generous	inspiring
broad-minded	deep-thinking	genuine	integrity
candid	deliberate	giving	intense
capable	demanding	grateful	inventive
character	dependable	gregarious	involved

---

* Losoncy, L., *The Motivating Leader,* New York: Prentice-Hall, 1985, pp. 71–73.

judicious
kind
knowledgeable
leadership
learned
likable
loyal
merciful
moral
motivated

motivator
negotiable
organized
outstanding
participator
peaceful
perceptive
persevering
persistent

persuasive
positive
powerful
precise
productive
purposeful
realistic
reliable
responsible

self-confident
sensitive
team worker
thorough
thoughtful
visionary
watchful
wholehearted
wise

15. PARTICIPATIVE MANAGEMENT EVALUATION

My perception of participative management in my company

4 = Always   3 = Often   2 = Sometimes   1 = Seldom

_____ 1. The participative management style encourages ownership thinking at all levels of the company.

_____ 2. Participative management provides an attitude of trust and respect which prevails at all levels.

_____ 3. Participative management develops goals that are aligned and mutually acceptable and that lead to specific results.

_____ 4. Organizational goals are clearly stated, understood, and accepted by everyone.

_____ 5. Roles, goals, and responsibilities are clearly delineated.

_____ 6. Each person takes full responsibility for his or her actions, which may have consequences both positive and negative.

_____ 7. Work and discipline are self-directed, but in line with team expectations and corporate goals.

_____ 8. Emphasis is on the solving of problems rather than the placing of blame.

_____ 9. Brainstorming sessions stimulate creativity, contributions, and involvement.

_____ 10. Everyone is involved in developing and planning. There is little competition between people and departments.

_____ 11. Cooperation and teamwork are the route to success. Every leader and every associate is involved in improving the company.

_____ 12. There is open expression of ideas and open participation in decision making.

_____ 13. Suggestions frequently flow from all areas of the company. Suggestions are expected, welcomed, evaluated, and acted upon as appropriate.

_____ 14. Participants feel that they are heard instead of that their input must be accepted and acted upon.

_____ 15. Everyone is educated in the key aspects of the organization. Information is shared regularly about the company as a whole and each department.

_____ 16. There is communication up, down, and sideways. Communication is for the purpose of improving situations and relationships.

_____ 17. Feedback to leaders is encouraging as well as challenging.

_____ 18. Leaders do not feel threatened by staff participation and involvement. Leaders' decisions are open to scrutiny.

_____ 19. Managers at all levels of the company are seen as leaders interested in each employee's success and development.

_____ 20. Change is considered a way of life on the road to progress. Stability comes from learning to regard change as constant.

_____ 21. Problem areas are seen as opportunities and possibilities to apply expertise and develop alternatives.

_____ 22. The focus is on the end result as achieved by the total team and measured by corporate goals.

_____ 23. The work atmosphere is characterized by courage, risk taking, responsibility, and accepting the consequences of one's actions.

_____ 24. Work is accomplished through cooperation in an encouraging, positive atmosphere.

_____ 25. Participative management fosters and creates an environment in which varied opinions, ideas, experiences, and creativity are shared to produce not only a feeling of involvement, but also participation in creating excellence.

Through an item analysis, leaders can determine areas in which there are particular problems and identify strengths in their participative management program.

16. GUIDELINES FOR EVALUATING ENCOURAGING LEADERS

How can you become an encouraging leader? You can begin by recognizing and owning your own potential. Then you will be more aware of opportunities to encourage others.

The following guidelines will establish a process for assessing your current status and goals. After each point, indicate whether (1) you believe the statement is a strength of yours, (2) you are adequate, or (3) your need to improve.

	(1) *Strength*	*(2)* *Adequate*	*(3) Need* *Improvement*
1. I identify challenges and opportunities rather than problems.			
2. I identify the positive potential in people and in many situations.			
3. I am solution oriented.			
4. I focus on strengths and manage weaknesses.			
5. I inventory assets—I think of others in terms of their strengths.			
6. I remind people of their strengths.			
7. I establish and align goals between the organization and the employee.			
8. I appraise performance with positive performance reviews.			

	(1) Strength	(2) Adequate	(3) Need Improvement
9. I employ choices and consequences.			
10. I communicate openly and frequently.			
11. I move away from a unilateral evaluation role and have employees become more self-evaluative.			
12. I encourage employees to develop internal expectations and help them become their dreams, hopes, and goals.			
13. I spend considerable time listening to people. I hear the whole message.			
14. I have a positive ("I know something good about you") optimistic attitude.			
15. I make a conscious effort to point out what employees do right.			
16. I help each employee appreciate the relevance of his or her contribution.			
17. I treat everyone equally with regard to mutual respect and dignity.			

	(1) Strength	(2) Adequate	(3) Need Improvement
18. I see hidden assets and re- sources in employees and spotlight them.			
19. I help reframe perceived negative shortcomings into positive strengths.			
20. I give recognition for effort and improvement instead of only for the finished task.			

OTHER TITLES OF INTEREST FROM ST. LUCIE PRESS

The Skills of Encouragement: Bringing Out the Best in Yourself and Others

Real Dream Teams

Problem Solving for Results

Focused Quality: Managing for Results

Mastering the Diversity Challenge: Easy On-the Job Applications for Measurable Results

The Motivating Team Leader

Creating Productive Organizations: Manual and Facilitator's Guide

Organizational Teams: Building Continuous Quality Improvement

Team Building: A Structured Learning Approach

Healthcare Teams: Building Continuous Quality Improvement

Creating Quality in the Classroom

Teams in Education: Creating an Integrated Approach

For more information about these titles call, fax or write:

St. Lucie Press
100 E. Linton Blvd., Suite 403B
Delray Beach, FL 33483
TEL (407) 274-9906 • FAX (407) 274-9927

$S{\overset{t}{L}}$